The Compleat Manager
What Works When

Alan C. Filley

RESEARCH PRESS COMPANY
2612 North Mattis Avenue
Champaign, Illinois 61820

Copyright © 1978 by Alan C. Filley

All rights reserved. Printed in the United States of America. No part of this book may be reproduced by mimeograph or any other means without the written permission of the publisher. Excerpts may be printed in connection with published reviews in periodicals without express permission.

Copies of this book may be ordered from the publisher at the address given on the title page.

Second printing 1979

ISBN 0-87822-184-0

Library of Congress Catalog Card Number: 78-62907

Acknowledgments

Just as proper food for the body makes it function better, proper food for the intellect seems to make it work more effectively, too. My intellect and knowledge have been nourished by being around many talented people. Most immediately, there are my colleagues. Ray Aldag, Larry Cummings, and George Huber, in particular, have enriched my understanding of management, almost from day to day. Then, there are those who forego empty academic posturing in favor of real discovery and application: Robert House, Victor Vroom, Ed Lawler, Norman Maier, Ed Locke, and Jay Galbraith are prominent in that regard.

I am also indebted to the thousands of chief executives in medium-sized businesses with whom I have had contact. Being in a position to apply managerial knowledge to their firms and to suffer the consequences if it was not appropriate, they have forced me to be clear and substantive. They also have provided me with the benefit of their own knowledge and wisdom.

My thanks also go to Bob Parkinson, Rick Stephens, Ann Wendel, and Russ Pence at Research Press who have enough confidence in this unusual book to publish it. Finally, I am grateful to those who have listened to me, particularly my wife Florence.

... in ancient times a debate hath risen, and it remains yet unresolved, whether the happiness of man in this world doth consist more in contemplation or action? Concerning which, some have endeavoured to maintain their opinion of the first; by saying, that the nearer we mortals come to God by way of imitation, the more happy we are. And they say, that God enjoys Himself only by a contemplation of his own infiniteness, eternity, power, and goodness, and the like. And upon this ground, many cloisteral men of great learning and devotion, prefer contemplation before action. And many of the fathers seem to approve this opinion, as may appear in their commentaries ....

And on the contrary, there want not men of equal authority and credit, that prefer action to be the more excellent; as namely, experiments in physick, and the application of it, both for the ease and prolongation of man's life; by which each man is enabled to act and do good to others, either to serve his country, or do good to particular persons: and they say also, that action is doctrinal, and teaches both art and virtue, and is a maintainer of human society; and for these, and other like reasons, to be preferred before contemplation.

Concerning which two opinions I shall forbear to add a third, by declaring my own; and rest myself contentedly in telling you, my very worthy friend, that both these meet together, and do most properly belong to the most honest, ingenuous, quiet, and harmless art of angling.

Izaak Walton, The Compleat Angler

Contents

Acknowledgments iii
Preface vii

1 Learning to Ask
What Works When   1

2 The Effects of Organization   9

3 Types of Organization—
The Craft Type   15

4 Types of Organization—
The Promotion Type   23

5 Types of Organization—
The Administrative Type   31

6 Leadership   45

7 Motivation of Others   65

8 Decision Making and
Problem Solving   81

9 A Road Map for Decision
Making   101

10 Managing Your Time—
    Analysis and Control   115

11 Managing Your Time—
    Tips for Time-Saving   133

12 Designing Your Organization—
    Two Structures   149

13 Designing Your
    Organization—Some
    Key Dimensions   169

14 Job Design   191

15 Selecting Good People   205

16 Finding Resources
    and Advice   219

    Epilog   231
    Notes   233
    About the Author   239

Preface

There is an instruction book on fly-fishing[1] that begins by directing the reader to, first, catch a fish. That is, instead of mystifying the reader with the complexities of fly-fishing—rods, reels, lures, lines, water, weather, casting, and the like—the book says to get a 7½-foot rod, a reel 3 1/4 inches in diameter, a size D floating line, some leaders, and half a dozen artificial flies. Then, it says to find a farm pond containing bluegills and bass and experience the success of catching a fish in one evening.

This kind of start into fly-fishing is wonderfully helpful. The directions are clear, and the odds are that the new fisherman is likely to succeed immediately with his efforts. This gives him confidence that a complicated sport can be learned by dealing first with information which is likely to have the most impact. Having learned the basics and having demonstrated their success, the fisherman can begin fine-tuning his skills and knowledge.

In writing this book I have tried to do the same thing. Unlike most books on management, including my own,[2] which provide detailed information about the various dimensions of management, this present treatment tries to provide the skills which will have an immediate impact on managerial performance. If it succeeds in doing so, you, the reader, should gain confidence in the fact that management can be learned and that academic knowledge is not something remote from the real world.

I also have written in a personal style, telling personal experiences and anecdotes. Such methods of conveying information are common in Eastern traditions for instruction, including early Christian and Judaic sources, and they make learning an immediate, real, pleasant process. I hope that my own use of this approach is similarly useful and enjoyable.

There is much information which is necessary for managerial success which is not contained here. Good managers have an enormous assortment of knowledge and skill. They have financial, technical, or other functional knowledge appropriate to their particular positions. They also have the wisdom which is probably gained by experience rather than from books. What is offered to the reader in this volume is some basic information which should make managers in many different settings *more effective.*

*Chapter 1 Learning to Ask
What Works When*

In the discovery of secret things and in the investigation of hidden causes, stronger reasons are obtained from sure experiments and demonstrated arguments than from probable conjectures and the opinions of philosophical speculators of the common sort.

William Gilbert (1600)

Promoter or Manager

In 1951 I became a salesman and later sales manager for a small retail music store and studio in central Illinois. The business had just been purchased by a young man, Gene Harris, from members of his family. It had operated with little growth and no particular success in a small, rented storefront near the downtown area of the city. The music shop sold a variety of instruments, and the owners gave music lessons to about twenty-five students.

Harris had recently graduated from college and was without much money. He lived in a small apartment, drove an old car, and paid for the business out of earnings. Five years later, this same business claimed 1500 students taking accordion lessons, had 75 small branch studios around the Midwest, sponsored an hour-long television program, operated out of its own building, and by many measures was successful and profitable. Harris now had a large home and his own airplane and managed the largest retail accordion business in the Midwest.

I worked for Harris for four years and during that time took courses and read books about how to manage. In reading books about management I discovered that what Harris was doing was largely the opposite of what the books said one should do to run a successful business. My first thought was, "Well, it just goes to show you that the people who write those books don't know anything about the real world. They've never met a payroll." Then I thought, "Well, it can't be that simple; maybe what we are doing in the music business is just an exception, and what the books say is generally right." Finally, it occurred to me that maybe what Harris was doing was right in one phase of business life and what the books said was right in another phase.

The difficulty with this explanation was that the books didn't say *when* their advice was correct and when it wasn't, and none of us knew enough about Harris' way of doing business to say why it worked when it did. It has taken me seventeen years of research, consulting, and thought to get an approximate answer to the simple question, "What works when?" Added to that effort is an enormous amount of research by others, beginning mainly in the 1950s, which has provided understanding and practical tools for business management. Unfortunately, much of such wisdom is unknown to practicing managers, even those with formal education, simply because it is buried in sophisticated research reports, complicated theories, and a morass of academic rhetoric.

More on that point later. To finish the story of Gene Harris and his music enterprise—the business grew like a skyrocket for five years, then reversed itself, plummeting down like a burned-out skyrocket for two more years. Finally, it closed its doors. The puzzling thing at the time was the fact that during the decline it was doing exactly what it had been doing before. Harris then tried a number of other ventures. He started a go-cart track which paid for itself in a couple of years. He invested in oil wells. He bought a firm manufacturing church furniture. Then, he obtained the patent for a rotary lawn mower and went into the mower manufacturing business. The mower was unique in having one wheel at the rear on a swivel instead of the usual two fixed wheels. It swiveled around trees just fine, but never would go in a straight line very well.

Knowing very little about manufacturing and having to compete with lots of others in the market, Harris had trouble. It cost him as much to make his brand as the retail price of his competitors' mowers that were sold in department stores. Not to be outdone, Harris tried loading his mowers on trucks and selling them directly on market day in small towns. As might be expected, this business was terminated. Eventually, I lost contact with Harris, but acquaintances said that he owned another music business for a while and left that to start a company making display charts for chiropractors.

While working on this book I heard from Harris again. He wrote to say that he had seen a brochure for my workshop on managing the smaller, rapidly growing manufacturing firm. His letter indicated that he now owns a company which makes exercise equipment.

It is clear from Harris' history that he was and perhaps still is a promoter rather than a manager. As far as I know, he has never developed the skills of management, though I believe he could if he wanted to. His style is that of a starter or builder of business, and it appears that he chooses to get out of the business once the opportunities for promotion have ended. In contrast, this book will suggest how to build a stable base for further growth, once the advantage of the first promotion is past. To do so requires a different form of leadership and a different form of business organization.

Two things characterized Harris' early success in the music business. First, the business was innovative. The growth was based on a simple plan of going to small towns, putting on a music show in the grade schools, and then calling on all the children in their homes to register them for a ten-week trial on the accordion. The instrument was furnished for the trial period—they paid only for the lessons—and a teacher was sent to the community. Once the trial ended, the students purchased their own instruments or quit. We enrolled students before they were old enough for school band classes, and our instruction was generally the only opportunity for music lessons without traveling long distances to large cities.

The second characteristic of Harris' business success seemed to be his own personal charisma. Everyone associated with him was excited about the possibilities for personal success and enrichment that association with him could provide. There was personal attraction to a leader who seemed to be gifted with talents that others simply didn't have. For a time, everyone was living his own "impossible dream." As I will discuss later, such charisma is the stuff that crusades are made of—whether in business, as with Durant at General Motors; in revolutions, as with Castro in Cuba; or in religious movements, as with Jesus.

The Author's Experience and Biases

My own career eventually became academic. After Army, graduate school, and early teaching experience, I joined the faculty of a large state university. Sixteen years as an academician have, I hope, provided the substance of knowledge and the wisdom of experience. In addition, for about ten years I have given seminars for chief executives of small or medium-sized manufacturing and retail firms and have consulted with a number of such firms. Most of my experience is with companies having sales of roughly half a million dollars to six million. Since 95 percent of the firms in this country have fewer than twenty employees, I think that companies in the half million to six million dollar size range are often the real successes in enterprise.

While I'm talking about biases, let me suggest a few more. First, to the reader who is currently in a paid management position, be it president or department manager, I really don't want to suggest that I can do your job as well as you can right now. You probably have a great many skills that I lack. On the other hand, I doubt that many practicing managers could do my job as well as I can. I have the time, the training, and the research skills to study what successful managers do that unsuccessful managers don't do. One job is no more important than the other—the two are simply different.

I dwell on this because of all the seemingly foolish discussions about whether business people with all their practical experience shouldn't be teaching business and whether professors wouldn't be more effective if they had run a business. I doubt it. Business people and business professors are simply two different specialists who should understand each other's roles and benefit from each other. I don't expect my physician to have had my illnesses.

Given this realization, we might be spared the information provided regularly by executives who write books about management. Instead of describing their own experience and providing useful descriptive information, such writers sometimes embark on prescriptions about how to be successful which may not be grounded in fact. Two exceptions come to mind. The first is a book by J. Paul Getty, *How To Be A Successful Executive*[1] which, though not academically sophisticated, at least is honest and not wrong in what it says. Getty's book does not suggest that one fire the advertising agency, nor does it provide a lengthy list of leadership traits, as do many such books. The other book is Chester Barnard's

The Functions of the Executive.[2] Originally published in 1938 and followed by later editions, Barnard's book shines as a profound, seminal contribution to management theory.

Another of my biases is the belief that there are no magic formulas which will make a business or a manager successful. The odds favoring success can be improved with skill and hard work. There is a seemingly endless list of fads: scientific management, human relations, brainstorming, critical path scheduling, program budgeting, transactional analysis, management by objectives, sensitivity training—add your own. Used improperly, as magic cures, they are at best worthless and at worst destructive. Improving management skills might be compared to doing physical exercise. Vigorous exercise programs can make amazing changes in physiology and even mental health, but they require effort to accomplish; the result is improvement, not a magic cure.

Preview

In the chapters which follow, I will try to provide a practicing or potential manager with some basic tools of his trade. Some of the information here is from my own research; much is from the work of others. All of it, though, originates from studying the practices of real managers, comparing the difference between what successful and unsuccessful managers do. In addition, since successful practices vary in different situations, I will pay particular attention to the issue of what works when.

Chapter 2   The Effects of Organization

Do you know, my son, with what little understanding the world is ruled?

To a Portuguese monk who sympathized with the Pope's burden of office — Julius III

Prologue of a Parable
To begin our discussion of management practices, I'd like to tell an imaginary story. My reason for doing this is to show the purpose of getting things organized and the different effects that organization can have on people. For some reason, people associate policies and organization structures with bureaucracy and red tape. Used properly, however, such organizing tools can actually give people more freedom to do their jobs and can make them more effective.

The story which follows[1] illustrates the use of rules in three ways: as obstacles to freedom because they are inflexible and not understood; as barriers to efficiency because they change at the whim of the leader; and as useful tools in creating freedom and effective action for members of an organization.

The Parable of the Traffic Light:
Uses and Misuses of Rules*
There is in Colorado a small town, Goldline, home of 1,300 citizens, which started when the mines in that area were active. J. P. Goldsmith, owner of the Goldline and Colorado Railroad, is credited as its founder though he never chose to live there. Goldsmith helped the town to grow when he put in the rail line to serve the mines; and the grade school, bank, and hotel still bear his name. His nephew is mayor of Goldline today, and the town council includes two distant relatives.

In 1920 J. P. Goldsmith himself visited the town to celebrate the opening of the new school. After the necessary speeches and ribbon cutting, Goldsmith drove to the hotel. This hotel was located at the corner of Broad and High Streets at the center of the town and one block from the railroad station. Gazing fondly at his city from his room in the hotel, Goldsmith was struck with an idea. "By God," he said, "what this town needs is a traffic light right here at the

---

*From "The Parable of the Traffic Light" by A. C. Filley. *MSU Business Topics,* Vol. 24, No. 4, 1976. Used with permission.

corner of Broad and High."

So it was, in that very year, that the citizens of Goldline were surprised to find a traffic light in the center of their town. The mayor explained to the townspeople that the light was a gift from Goldsmith himself and that it was there to improve the operation of the town. He emphasized that when the light showed red, all traffic was to stop, and when the light showed green, traffic was to proceed. Once installed, however, the light failed to switch from red to green. For traffic on High Street the light was always green, and for the traffic on Broad Street the light was always red.

Since no one wanted to bother Goldsmith with trifles and because no one in the town knew how to repair it, the light remained permanently red to Broad Street traffic. And so it does today. In consequence, traffic must avoid travel on Broad Street at the corner. Because of this, the hotel is inconvenient to reach and its business has declined. The center of town has shifted several blocks away.

Yet the people of Goldline do not question the existence of the light. It is part of the town's tradition. In fact, if anyone be so bold as to move through the red light, he is held to be of questionable character and mildly sinful.

What Happened at Hillbottom
Not 200 miles from Goldline, in the center of a mountain range, is another town, Hillbottom, Colorado. Hillbottom began when a syndicate of businessmen and dentists in Denver saw the growing interest in winter sports and built the town as a vacation center for skiers. Condominiums were built and almost overnight, it seemed, restaurants, shops, golf courses, and other businesses were started.

Much of the credit for Hillbottom's success goes to Jake Hill, who saw the opportunity, gathered together the financial support from businessmen and dentists, and moved to Hillbottom to manage the construction of his town. Quite naturally, the citizens elected Hill as the first mayor and he served in that capacity until 1970.

One of the improvements to Hillbottom introduced by Jake Hill was the addition of one, then two, then three traffic lights at major intersections. So involved with such traffic matters was Hill that he decided personally each day whether the red meant stop or whether, on that particular day, red meant go while green meant stop. In the early days, with only one or two thousand people in Hillbottom, the matter was handled rather easily by a telephone call to Hill's office every morning to ask whether the red meant stop or go on that day. In fact, to provide service to guests, the managers of the condominium complexes would call for their residents and then post a sign in the lobby. As the population grew, however, Hill was forced to add additional telephone lines and was heard on several occasions to complain that if the people in the town weren't so dependent on his leadership he would have given up being mayor to work on other projects. Then, too, there were other problems with uninformed tourists who would come to town for the first time and *assume* that red meant stop. Serious traffic accidents were not unknown. Following each, Hill would complain to the people in City Hall, "Dammit, fellows, don't people know that they have to check with me every day?"

Finally, in December of 1970, Hill himself fell victim to the danger. An orthodontist from Nebraska drove through a green light and wrapped Hill and his red Porsche around a concrete hotel sign. The town council met the following day and decided that the mayor's office would be handled by a city manager. They identified the duties expected in the job and the criteria to be used in selection. In particular, they wanted someone with demonstrated competence in the functions of a city manager since the best predictor of future behavior is past behavior in a similar situation. Within a month, they had interviewed candidates and were fortunate in finding the ideal person, Harold Collins, who had served as a successful manager in another ski area and who knew Hillbottom from previous visits.

One of Collins' first actions was to declare that from then on the red lights would mean stop. A few residents who had grown used to the old system called to make sure that Collins meant *every day,* but most expressed relief at the new system. With an established pattern at the stoplights people could predict each other's behavior and their actions were coordinated. The only complaint came from a retired periodontist who was heard to say that the new system was too impersonal.

The consensus of townspeople was, however, that their time was better used on other matters instead of calling each day to find out whether the red light meant stop or go.

Epilogue of a Parable
This story emphasizes two things: first, that people who work together have more freedom if they know what to expect from each other; and second, that when repeated activities can be made efficient, people can use their energy and resources for matters that are not routine and that require their creative effort.

The story also describes three different settings in which rules were either traditional, arbitrary, or tools for coordinating action. These three settings are described in more detail in the next three chapters, discussing the craft, promotion, and administrative forms of organization.

Chapter 3 Types of Organization — The Craft Type

Wist ye not that I must be about my Father's business?

Luke 2:49

Three Types of Organization
The story about Goldline and Hillbottom in Chapter 2 suggests three quite different approaches to leadership and organization. In Goldline, leadership was strongly determined by social status rather than by selection for a defined position from among a number of possible candidates. In Hillbottom, under Jake Hill, leadership was based on personal control over the town by a man with promotion skills. The final leader of Hillbottom, Harold Collins, was a professional manager skilled in his job and chosen by formal selection procedures.

The traffic light represented an organizing method in each situation. In the first, the traffic light embodied tradition and, although it served no useful purpose, was maintained even at a cost. In the second, the traffic light required interpretation by Jake Hill at a cost of his own time and effort. In the third, it merely provided a means for members of the town to anticipate each other's actions. It provided coordinated effort with a minimal expenditure of time.

To look at such differences more directly, let's consider three types of organization which we can call the *craft type,* the *promotion type,* and the *administrative type.* Although every organization probably contains some characteristics of all three, experience indicates that one type is likely to be dominant in any organization, whether it be a dry cleaning establishment, a metal fabricating firm, or a city government. In this and the following two chapters, I shall try to give some of the flavor of these types. These descriptions are not meant to be proof, for an example is never a proof, but they do illustrate the nature of each.

The Craft Organization

Objectives and Policies
Imagine yourself, then, walking into a craft-type of firm and asking the leader a series of questions. You ask, "What are your objectives?" The leader will likely respond, "Well, I want to make a good living. I want to send my kids to school. I want money in the bank. I want to see the business sur-

vive." "But," you ask, "how do you determine your success?" He responds, "Look, we've been in business for forty-five years and have made a profit every year." Since the median business life is roughly seven to eight years, by this measure you might judge him to be quite successful. If you ask, "What do you want for the future?" the likely response is "More of the same."

"What are your policies?" you ask. He says, "I don't know what you mean by policy." You respond, "Well, if I work for you and use my car for company business, how many cents a mile do I get for reimbursement? What happens if I spit on the floor? How many paid holidays do I get? Who is my boss? What are my job standards? How does someone get promoted around here?" The craftsman responds, "Well, you have to pick up that stuff by experience."

The craftsman's reliance on experience combined with the fact that he doesn't believe that other people can give him much useful information about how to run his business can be both a strength and a weakness. It is a strength because experience seems to generate a sort of intuitive wisdom which one cannot obtain from books or education. It is a weakness because it may prevent him from adjusting his business operations as conditions change. To suggest the difficulty of experience, there is reason to believe that, contrary to folklore, one does not become rigid and conservative and uncreative with age. Those characteristics may relate more closely to the amount of time one has spent doing the same thing. In some occupations, creative skills peak out in about six years, requiring change and new information if the person is to be creative and adaptive.[1] This suggests to me that youthfulness in thinking and behavior depends more on change than on physical aging.

In the case of the craftsman, if he has been doing the same thing for more than six years, he may be so fixed in his behavior and beliefs that he cannot change even though it is required for the success of the company.

An example of this tendency toward rigidity may be seen in cases where a person acquires an ongoing organization which he is expected to lead. Again, popular folklore suggests that when a person obtains an organization, he must bring in his own executive team if changes are to be made. The reason for this belief may well be that new business owners have asked the existing plant manager why the plant layout is so strange, only to be told, "Well, sir, I know you're the new owner and all, but our business is unique, and this system works particularly well for us." What the man may actually be responding is, "We've done it for ten years this way, and we hate to change." An alternative to bringing in a new executive team would be reorganizing the situation so that people have new responsibilities and reporting relationships. In such cases, they will seek help, which may be provided by the new business leader.

Structure in Terms of Power Levels

The structure in the craft firm is arranged into levels of power. The top level contains what I prefer to call the *official family*. These are individuals who are in the elite because they are blood relatives, relatives by marriage, or people about whom the craftsman says, "She's like my own daughter," or "He's like my own son." Such individuals may be highly skilled, but the important point is that they are in their positions of leadership not because of a selection process for a defined job, but rather because of accidents of birth or friendship or marriage.

The second level in the craft organization I would call the *trusted-employee group*. These are the long-service people to whom the official family has given some supervisory responsibility. These trusted employees who have been rewarded for their long service and loyalty may not, however, function well as supervisors even though they are skilled in whatever operation is involved. They may be reluctant to share their knowledge with subordinates if doing so means that they have less power and prestige in the company. These monopolies of power can be costly to an organization since such individuals are viewed as indispensable or irreplaceable and have greater bargaining power with their bosses.

The third level in the craft firm may be characterized as a *transient group*. There is generally a high turnover among such lower-level employees, but those who do remain may eventually drift into the trusted-employee group.

De-emphasis of Supervisory Function
Craft firms are reluctant to employ people in supervisory or staff specialist positions. There are relatively few people with supervisory responsibilities, and they may spend much of their time doing work similar to that of their subordinates. Since the operations are stable, people acquire skills over time and probably don't require the degree of planning and control provided by staff specialists in a changing organization.

Concentration of Efforts
Craft firms in manufacturing generally concentrate their efforts in production activities rather than in sales, finance, or engineering. The firm may have a niche in the local market or an established reputation such that clients bring their business to the organization. In much the same way, people in this country prior to 1840 would go to a shoemaker or a carpenter to have their shoes or cabinets made. In other cases, an organization may be primarily engaged in selling, just as one sold pots off a wagon in early days.

Level of Morale
If you investigate the level of morale in a craft firm, you will rarely find serious problems. One source of dissatisfaction is the difference between one's expectations and one's accomplishments. If a person expects to have a color television set and doesn't get one, she may be dissatisfied. If the person doesn't expect one and doesn't get one, she is not dissatisfied. Since the craft firm does not create expectations for promotion or job change and since it is likely to buy the same materials from the same sources, produce in the same way, and sell to the same customers year after year, its employees are not likely to be dissatisfied. They have pretty much what they expect to have.

Tendency Away from Innovativeness
Craft firms are not likely to be innovative. They may display a high degree of skill within their established technology, but they are not likely to try things which require new kinds of knowledge. For example, I recall interviewing the owner of a hardware store in the Midwest. The store had dusty, empty bins, an oiled wooden floor, incandescent bulbs, and decidedly old-fashioned fixtures. I asked the owner whether he was a member of the local hardware dealers association which had a model store and was highly regarded in that area. He said, "No. My business is unique because, you see, I still sell some pump fixtures to people in this neighborhood."

Dependence on Benevolent Environment
The owner of the craft firm operates as if he has perfect knowledge upon which to make his decisions. He is not likely to take risks. He is not a gambler, and he operates in the pattern that he has grown used to. In that sense, then, the craft organization depends upon a benevolent environment. That is, it doesn't *act upon* its environment, and it doesn't respond to changes in the environment. If customers choose to continue to buy its products and its competitive situation does not change, the craft firm may continue to prosper. On the other hand, if its clients change their interests, then the craft firm may suffer without really knowing why.

I recall a craft-type retail furniture company which I interviewed some years ago that sold high-quality furniture on credit. The composition of the neighborhood had changed and the average income level had dropped sharply. The furniture store continued to sell high-quality furniture on credit, but its bad debt losses were so high that it was losing money. When I asked the owner what he was doing about the situation, he complained about the irresponsible people who lived in the neighborhood and said that the government gave all the benefits to the farmers and not to the small businessmen. He did not discuss possible changes in his product line or in his credit policies or in the location of the store. He didn't adapt at all. In contrast, at about the same time I interviewed the owner of a small appliance repair shop located near the downtown area of the same city. For years the shop had repaired items such as razors, toasters, and irons brought in by customers. The owner realized the change in his own neighborhood and in customer buying habits. He said, "At one time the housewife would be given an iron when she got married and would have it repaired when it broke down. Now she goes to the local discount house and buys a new iron. I've got to be as convenient to the housewife as the local discount store." With that in mind, he kept records on population by district in the city, traffic patterns in the city, and construction of shopping centers. He was developing a variety of alternatives that would permit him to adapt to the new situation. Now he has a series of pickup stations located in various parts of the city, which are as convenient as the discount house.

Depending on the nature of its environment, a craft firm might grow, but more often its level of operations remains relatively stable. This situation need not be unfavorable if the craft firm has a secure position with an established clientele which permits it to maintain a profitable operation.

Chapter 4 Types of Organization — The Promotion Type

[John Y. Brown, promoter of Kentucky Fried Chicken, and Lums,] "... says he got a kick out of seeing Kentucky Fried grow, but managing it after it got big was another matter. 'When we got past a couple hundred million dollars in sales I knew I needed help, so I called in some so-called professional managers,' he relates. 'You never saw a more negative bunch. Those guys came in with textbooks under their arms telling us all the things we weren't supposed to be doing. If I'd have listened to them in the first place, we'd never have started Kentucky Fried Chicken. It got to be no fun, so I got out.' "

Others close to the company see this situation somewhat differently. They say that in engineering Kentucky Fried's explosive growth, Mr. Brown neglected to install needed financial controls and food-research facilities, and had let relations with some franchise-holders go sour. Those factors contributed to the stock's plunge from its peak of about $55 a share in 1969—against an initial 1966 offering price of just over $2, allowing for splits—to about $22 a share at the time of the merger [with Heublein, Inc.]. They say the merger came at the right time, and under Heublein the company's growth has resumed on sounder footing.

Wall Street Journal, April 1, 1975, p. 19.

Objectives and Policies
If you interview the chief executive of a promotion type of business, asking the same questions that you asked the craft leader just described, you are likely to hear quite different responses. When you say to the leader, "What are your objectives?" she is likely to say something like—"I want to shoot for the moon," or "I want to make a million dollars." One man said, "Filley, do you see that parking lot out there?" I said "Yes." He said, "That's the employee parking lot, and our objective is to see that lot full of pink Cadillacs." As you would discover, such objectives make people excited about the future.

The usefulness of objectives may be illustrated as follows: Suppose that Jones would like to start a revolution. He gathers a group together and says, "Look, folks, I'm planning on starting this revolution. Now, we're all going to have to make sacrifices. We're going to live in the woods and eat bugs and sleep on the ground, and hopefully when we get through—if we can win this revolution—everyone will be better off." I wouldn't join a revolution like that, and neither would you. On the other hand, if Jones says to the group, "What is it we'd all like? What is our dream? Each of us would like his own piece of land, right? And who has the land? Those bad guys—those landowners. Well, you follow me in the revolution, and I promise you everyone's going to have his own piece of land. Now, we may have to sacrifice a bit—we'll sleep in the woods and eat a few bugs. But when it's over, everyone will have his own piece of land." Perhaps we might be tempted to join that revolution. The dreams and expectations in the promotion organization—whether for riches, power, achievement, happiness, or perfect peace—tend to raise people's expectations and unify them in their excitement.

If you ask the leader, "What are your policies?" he, like the craftsman, may respond, "What do you mean?" You say, "Well, if I work here, how do I know how many cents per mile I get if I use my car for company business, or what happens if I spit on the floor, or how do I get promoted, or what is my job, or how many paid holidays do I get?" The promotion leader is likely to answer, "Oh, those things change from day to day. Whenever you want to know, you just ask me."

Leader's Position and Relationships
You are likely to conclude that the promotion leader is the central decision maker and central communication link for the whole organization. This strategy can be quite useful when conditions are changing daily, as may well be the case in the early years of a promotion-type organization, but it loses usefulness when conditions are stable enough or experience is well enough defined to permit more efficient policy and structure. For example, if I'm in the middle of a battle, with bullets whizzing by my head, I don't want a leader who says, "Gee, this is a new one on me. I'll have to look it up in the book." I want a leader who responds immediately and says, "Charge that hill." It's not surprising, then, that the structure in the promotion type is quite simple, with everyone reporting to the leader, at least in part. The organization may have job titles and levels of authority, but in fact the leader gets involved in everyone's job—telling the secretary when she can have a day off, the machine operator how to set up the machine, or the sweeper where to sweep. This structure also permits personal influence by the leader, an important element in maintaining her charisma with subordinates.

Promotion leaders with such a structure tend to cope with increasing demands on their time in several ways. First, they work longer and longer hours, spending evenings and weekends in the organization. Second, they put off any duties which do not have to be done immediately, causing less and less planning to be done when the opposite may actually be needed. Third, promotion leaders add "arms and legs" in the form of personal assistants. Such individuals may be identified as an assistant to, an executive secretary, or a right-hand person, but all serve as extensions of the leader herself. One day she may ask the assistant to take care of her correspondence and sign her name to it. Another day she may ask the assistant to go call on a supplier to find out why materials are late. In another case she may ask the assistant to find out the progress of a batch of work in process. A classic example of the promotion leader and the assistant-to's is Jesus. His twelve disciples, or seventy, depending on how you read your Bible, served as personal extensions of Jesus.

Emphasis on Different Functions

The promotion organization seems to emphasize different functions, all stemming from crises that develop as the organization grows. In a manufacturing firm, the major emphasis may first be on production. A company providing a desired product which is not available elsewhere needn't worry much about efficiency or selling, and so naturally it might expand production capability and number of production workers. But, selling may become an issue, so the company will deal with such matters as whether to change from manufacturing representatives to its own salespersons, whether to set up sales offices elsewhere, or how to compensate sales staff. Next, a company may find itself with a substantial level of sales, but relatively little profit, and so it will turn to preoccupation with budgeting and cost control. Later, it may be expected to add staff services, generally technical in nature, and finally to separate the administrative activities from the operational, day-to-day activities.

Level of Morale

Morale in the promotion firm tends to be very high early in the company's development and very low later in its experience. At first, everyone is turned on, with common high expectations about the rewards they will achieve. Later, it is not uncommon for a loss of long-service personnel to take place, for serious conflicts between the leader and the subordinates to develop, or for unionizing attempts to occur.

There seem to be several reasons for this crisis in morale later in the promotion type. First, the honeymoon is over. People discover that they will not have pink Cadillacs or be millionaires or have their own piece of land. Second, it appears that charismatic leaders tend to attract followers who feel that the leader will make their dreams come true. Such people probably go through life moving from one leader to another, one therapist to another, or one minister to another, searching for someone who will, in effect, lay hands on them and say, "Shazam, now you are OK," or happy, or wealthy, or whatever. They get disenchanted when they discover that their immediate leader is human after all and that the leader has no magic powers.

Finally, morale may be affected by the addition and utilization of middle-management levels in the organization. When employees who used to be actively involved with the charismatic promoter are asked to report to middle managers, they may become bitter or resentful. This is particularly true where the middle managers are new to the company. In Chapter 15 we will discuss how to minimize this problem, whether it occurs in the promotion type or in the other types.

Importance of Exploitation

Competitive Advantage
Initially, promotion companies invariably exploit the advantages of some kind of innovation. In addition, they are flexible, adaptive, and creative. The primary innovation upon which the business is based will be some distinct competitive advantage which will last for several years, providing the organization with a virtual monopoly for some period of time. The innovation may be a new market, a new method of distribution, a new source of supply, a new method of manufacturing, or anything that gives the company such a distinct advantage. Both the blessing and the curse of this position may be the fact that the organization need not be preoccupied with efficiency. No one needs to worry about nickels and pennies when the dollars are rolling in. The big problem occurs, however, when the company must begin to compete with other organizations, particularly on the basis of price.

For example, imagine the producer of a piece of industrial equipment which costs $20,000 to produce and sells for $60,000. The equipment doesn't work very well, but the purchaser finds that it pays for itself in a couple of years from savings once it is operational. Furthermore, suppose that this producer is the only source of the equipment in the market. Such a position can be deceptive if the producer feels that this utopia will continue forever. The company has no budgeting or cost control. The president is due to retire in two years. The sales manager has no salesmen reporting to him, and he is expected to retire along with the president. The purchasing, production scheduling and office and bookkeeping duties are carried out by one woman with a heroic effort. The company has no quality control. If I point out these and other problems to the president, he may say, "Sure, sure, Filley, we'll have to look into these things some day." What he means is, "Things are moving so fast and we're making so much money that those problems seem trivial." The next time I may hear from the president is when the company has lost a major order to a couple of new competitors who can produce the product more cheaply and whose product is more reliable.

Similarly, imagine the sole producer of hula hoops which cost, say, fifteen cents to make and sell for four dollars. Every kid in the country wants a hula hoop, and what parent is going to deny his child a four-dollar expense, particularly if every other kid in the neighborhood has a hula hoop. This is fine as long as it lasts, but what happens if a competitor appears who can sell hula hoops for fifteen cents *at a profit?* What happens is panic and crisis and an attempt to do things overnight which would have been better changed over a period of three or four years.

Type of Decision Making
The promotion firm makes decisions on the basis of uncertainty. The technical definition of uncertainty is an uncalculable probability of gain or loss. What this means is that circumstances are such that it is impossible to make a calculated, informed decision and that one must rely instead upon personal ability to deal with ambiguous conditions. Fortunately, the promotion leader typically has a high tolerance for ambiguity, a low fear of failure, and the ability to

make good decisions under such conditions.

Pattern of Growth
The basis for success of a promotion firm, then, is its exploitation of an innovation. Typically, this exploitation activity generates an S-shaped pattern of growth, with very rapid growth up to a point, after which increases in size occur at a decreasing rate. The slowing of growth near the end of the promotion period seems to occur for several reasons. One is the appearance of competitors in the market. Another is the saturation of the market in which it finds itself, particularly if it must reduce its premium pricing to reach a new market segment. Finally, promoters sometimes report that they simply got tired and could not keep up the pace any more. Whatever the reason, the promotion firm reaches a point of major vulnerability when, if it is to survive, it must change its type.

Historical Significance
Throughout history major changes in business, religion, government, unionization, or social structure have been through a promotion-type organization and its particular kind of leadership. Sometimes such changes destroyed older, traditional structures. In other cases, the promotion type initiated a new organization with no previous history. The skills required to promote a new institution are not the same as those required to sustain it, however. The promoter and the administrator do different things. Rarely, it seems, does the promoter also display the skills of the administrator.

Chapter 5 Types of Organization —
The Administrative Type

How can you be two places at once when you're not anywhere at all?

Firesign Theater

Objectives of Organization and Employees

If you now enter the administrative type of firm and ask the same set of questions you asked in the craft and promotion types, you will get a different pattern of responses. There are variations within the administrative pattern which are created by differences in technology or market environment or size, but the general pattern is clear.

If you ask the leader in the administrative organization for his objectives, the response will be specific plans for the future. The leader may say, "Well, our return on investment is planned at 25 percent. We expect to increase sales by 15 percent. Here are our sales and production budgets. Sales is broken down by units and dollars and includes the cost of sales budget. Production in units and dollars is broken down into direct labor, direct material, and factory overhead budgets. We expect to add two new products to our line. We will be adding three people in the sales department."

In other words, administrative objectives are stated as specific goals and plans. You may also discover in the administrative type that the goals of the institution are different from the goals of the members of the organization. Individuals want satisfaction of their personal needs and look upon the administrative organization as a place to work. Just as you or I might do, the salesperson in the administrative firm looks at his contributions to the organization; that is, how hard he works, his level of performance, his education, and other job-related characteristics and abilities that he brings to the job. He looks at the rewards that he gets for his performance—his pay, his work environment, his supervision, his job satisfaction, and the like—and then makes a comparison between his contributions and rewards here and those available in similar jobs in other organizations. He simply says to himself, "Do I get a better deal here or there?" Such behavior does not reflect greed or disloyalty; it is simply the general desire shared by all of us for satisfactory employment and a fair reward for our services.

If asked to identify what people want in their jobs, I like to report the research of Professor Fred Herzberg.[1] This information is only approximately correct for reasons which

I shall mention later. Herzberg has asked groups of people—initially accountants and engineers—to identify incidents that happened to them on the job which they found satisfying and to identify incidents on the job which they found dissatisfying. In addition, he asked them what effects such incidents had on them and how long the effects lasted. For example, a person might report that a good experience was receiving a promotion, that the effect was his decision that this is a good place to work, and that he still feels the same way.

When Herzberg analyzed such reports, he discovered that the categories associated with satisfying incidents were different from the categories associated with dissatisfying incidents. The dissatisfiers, or "hygiene factors," as he calls them, were most often incidents having to do with unfair company policy or administration, poor personal relations with the boss, poor technical supervision, unfair pay, and unsatisfactory working conditions. In contrast, the satisfying incidents, or "motivators," as he calls them, most often referred to recognition, personal achievement, opportunities for personal responsibility, interesting work, or advancement in the organization. For many types of employees, it is likely that the motivator category does relate to characteristics which increase job satisfaction. Herzberg claims that the hygiene factors can make people dissatisfied, but that they are not important sources of motivation. In a later discussion we will consider this point. For the present, however, Herzberg's findings do suggest the kinds of rewards which are desired by employees in the administrative type.

Independence from Personnel
Another characteristic of the administrative firm is its independence from the people within the organization. Within reason, administrative organizations have no indispensable people, including the leader. The potential for this kind of operation is illustrated in a water treatment company with which I have consulted. When I met the president in a training program, the company was clearly in the promotion stage. The president worked long hours, dealing with things

personally, but such efforts did not meet his needs. As a result of our description of the administrative type, the president returned home and reorganized the firm, changing it into an administrative structure. As a result, the president now spends three weeks out of every month working in the company and uses the other week each month to do other things which give him pleasure—sailing, traveling, vacationing. The company continues to grow and prosper. The difference is that the organization now works through prescribed goals and systems rather than depending upon the leader for day-to-day direction.

Policies to Promote Efficiency and Predictability
The policies in the administrative organization are simply guidelines which permit members to know what to expect from each other. If you say to the administrative leader, "What are your policies?" she is likely to hand you a company policy manual and an employee handbook, indicating the prescribed compensation for using one's car for company business, the consequences of disruptive actions, the boss-subordinate reporting relationships, the basis for promotion or compensation in the company, and other standards of behavior. Much like the traffic light at a busy corner, the policies simply permit individuals to engage in coordinated actions and to deal with nonroutine problems.

The effects of policies on people's feelings and actions in an organization may be further clarified as follows: If you ask large numbers of people whose work interacts with others how much freedom they *feel* they have in the job, as the amount of predictability in their jobs goes up, their felt freedom will probably increase and then decrease. In other words, suppose that you interview the employees in a company, asking them two questions. The first question is "On a scale from one to ten, where one is unpredictable and ten is very predictable, how would you rate your own job requirements?" Next, "On a scale from one to ten, where one is little felt freedom and ten is much felt freedom, how would you rate the degree of freedom that you feel in your own job?"

The results are likely to look like those in Figure 1.[2] A person at point A might be someone doing routine assembly work with a short, repetitive work cycle. It would not be surprising for such a person to state that he has very predictable job requirements and that his felt freedom in the job is low. In contrast, a person at point C might be someone whose boss is so capricious that it is impossible to predict from day to day exactly what the ground rules about job behavior are to be. That person might well report that he has little predictability in the job and that his felt freedom is quite low! Finally, a person at point B is likely to be someone whose job requirements are clear—with policies, clear goals, and a clear organizational structure—but not confining through adherence to a fixed work system. That person is likely to report moderate predictability in the job but higher felt job freedom than the person at point A or point C.

To be sure, the attitudes toward policy and structure will depend somewhat upon one's own personality and the work involved, but the general pattern described is common. In two social welfare agencies I recently heard employees complain because their agency heads were so busy and changed the job priorities of their subordinates so often that they simply could not take action on their own—they had little freedom. Ironically, the agency heads both complained because their subordinates could not think for themselves and take action without close supervision. The solution was simply to have the agency heads and their subordinates agree on policies and job priorities so that people could act with greater independence.

Structure—Planned and Emergent
The administrative structure will exist apart from the members of the organization. The job relationships, job content, departments, and levels of the organization are identified so that people know what to expect from each other and so that organization goals can be met most effectively. This is not to say that organization structures are not present unless they are planned. Any group of people working together will develop a structure. One will emerge. This emergent structure is

Figure 1. Predictability and Felt Freedom in the Job†

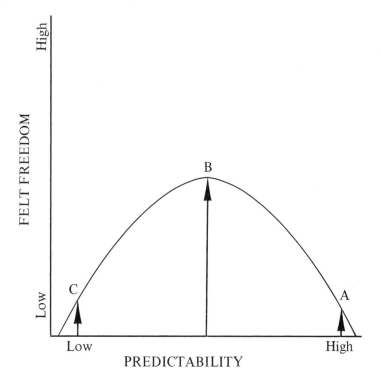

†Adapted from *Individual Behavior and Group Achievement* by R. M. Stogdill. Oxford: Oxford University Press, 1959.

not based on plans, and it's not based on the work to be performed. Instead, it is based very much upon the personal characteristics of the people involved. The difference between such an emergent structure and a planned structure is that the planned structure is based upon the needs of the organization. As will be discussed later, reliance on an unplanned, emergent structure can lead to the failure of an organization. In addition, an emergent structure may result in some people being considered indispensable; an organization pays a price for that. Such people might be identified as witch doctors. One witch doctor that I recall polished silicon wafers at the beginning of a three-month production cycle which ended in the creation of integrated circuits. Each year the employee would approach management saying, "Gee, I need more equipment," or "I really think I ought to be paid more." Since the employee was "indispensable," the response from management was more equipment or more pay. One day this same employee told management that he was quitting to take a trip around the world. As a result production was down for a month while people tried to figure out how the employee had been doing his job for the previous five years. Whether for reasons of eliminating witch doctors, providing efficiency of predictable behavior, or allowing a president to take a week out of every month for vacation, the planned structure clearly has benefits over the emergent structure.

Balance of Activities, Specialties
The administrative firm is one which adapts to the needs of its clients and its market. Unlike the craft firm which is dependent on a benevolent environment, or the promotion type which exploits its innovative advantage, the administrative type has leadership that moves carefully and deliberately by plan. One source of this planning, particularly in organizations which strive to maximize efficiency, is through employment of staff specialists. In manufacturing, these are people in jobs like production control, purchasing, inspection, personnel, accounting, cost control, and the like. For companies emphasizing long production runs with more than roughly 350 production employees, it is not unusual for such staff employment to be somewhere between 20 to 50 percent of production employment. As a smaller company grows from roughly 70 production employees to that size, the proportion of such specialists will increase rapidly. For companies which cannot afford such specialists I will suggest in Chapter 16 how to obtain outside help at relatively small expense.

The work performed in an administrative firm is balanced among the necessary activities involved. In manufacturing, this means that there will be a necessary balance between sales, production, and engineering activities. In retail, it might be sales, merchandising, and purchasing. As we will consider in a later chapter, these functions are grouped in two basic organizational strategies: One involves separate profit centers which stand more or less alone, and the other has all people doing the same kind of work grouped in the same department.

Level of Morale
Morale in the administrative structure may vary from good to bad, depending upon how people feel about their jobs and the organization. Unlike the promotion organization, in which people are joined together by mutual high expectations and informal relationships among everyone, the administrative firm generates its morale by providing individuals with rewards which they find satisfying and, in a more general way, by creating more common characteristics among organization members. Administrative firms do this in two ways: (1) by selection and (2) by indoctrination with the values of the organization. Management will select people whose needs and expectations fit the jobs and the climate provided by that particular institution. It will also make clear the beliefs and objectives of the organization so that members may either subscribe to those needs or find other employment.

Emphasis on Evolution Rather than Innovation
The administrative structure is characterized more by its emphasis on the development of its products or services than it is by major innovation. Changes in the administrative firm are made by careful planning rather than by plunging; products or services change gradually as market needs require, rather than dramatically through gambles on abrupt decisions. This administrative evolution is illustrated in the experience of a client of mine. When I first met him, I asked him what business he was in. He said, "I make a mud removal product." I said, "What do you mean?" He said, "Well, I make a product which removes the sediment from ballast tanks in Great Lakes ships. Great Lakes ships, unlike ocean vessels, use

water ballast. When the water is pumped in, the sediment settles in the bottoms of the tanks, and at one time people would climb into the tanks to chip the hardened sediment out of the bottom of the tanks. I make a polymer substance which fluidizes that sediment so that it can be pumped out of the tanks." Given this experience, he expanded his product line to provide sediment removal processes for sewage treatment and water-cooled engines. This, in turn, evolved into a full line of water treatment services, and this turned into a company identification of one which makes industrial chemicals.

Adaptation Through Risk Rather than Uncertainty
The administrative firm deals with risk rather than uncertainty. The technical definition of risk is a calculable probability of gain or loss; that is, the company knows the odds and builds the risk into its pricing structure or transfers it to an insurance carrier. Such planning and calculation is the job of staff services in the administrative structure. In much the same sense, the basis for success of the administrative firm is its planned adaptation to its environment. The administrative organization adjusts to the needs of its clients, expands its product base, and competes with other similar firms through efficient operation.

Administrative firms tend to grow over time. Their growth generally occurs through one of three sources: They expand within their established market, gaining more customers and sales; they move to new market areas; or they add related product lines within their realm of experience and planning.

Transition between Types
It is not uncommon for an organization to experience more than one type of operation during its lifetime. For example, a firm might start in the promotion type and then change into the administrative type. Or, it might start in the craft type and change into the administrative type. Any combination of all three types is possible.

When an organization moves from craft to promotion,

the change is abrupt, often taking place in a few weeks or months. The reason is simple: The personality of the leader in the craft organization is largely the opposite of the leader's personality in the promotion type. As we shall discuss in detail later, since personalities are not likely to change, a shift from craft to promotion will require a change in the chief executive. In addition, the change to promotion will contain an innovation and added financial investment to support the rapid growth of the promotion type.

In contrast, where the movement is from either the craft or the promotion type to the administrative type, the transition may occur over several years. Both the craft and the promotion types are strongly influenced by the top leader. The administrative type, on the other hand, is strongly dependent on systems of organization and control. Since administration is essentially the exercise of a set of *learned* skills, the question is more accurately, "Do you want to learn to be an administrator?" than it is, "Can you learn to be an administrator?"

Nor is the question, for promotion types, "Should we change to a new type?" In fact, the promotion organization *must* change or perish at some point. The promotion organization is one of transition; it is never permanent. Promotions—whether economic, social, political, or religious—must eventually change if they are to survive. The question is not "Shall we change?" The question is "Shall we change by deliberate planning or shall we change through crisis when our survival is threatened?"

The craft organization may also change to administration, but the reasons for doing so are less clear. Perhaps with a threat to survival, motivation to change is greater. Often, it seems, changes in the craft type occur through changes in leadership, whether through shifts in ownership or through succession of family control.

Since this discussion about transition may seem a bit abstract, let's take a real example of a firm which moved from the craft into the administrative type. The example involves Ken Homes, who owned a gasoline station, began specializing in muffler installation, and became an early franchiser of a shop to install mufflers.

He operated for several years in a small, two-stall location, working in one stall and his helper working in the other. So, Ken spent most of his time doing work like that of his subordinates. The subordinates were a transient group, starting and quitting over time. Ken made a reasonable living and could have continued in the same way for years, but he decided to change his method of operating. He moved into a new seven-stall location across from a local Sears store. At that point, he shifted from a craft to an administrative type. First, he trained the people in the shop to operate without his personal supervision. In order to stay out of the shop, Ken started wearing a white shirt to work, "because," he said, "my wife raises hell if I get grease on a white shirt."

Forced to stay in the front office, separating administration from operation, Ken found himself with time on his hands. Before the change, he had gone home tired after a full day's work. Now he had to find something to do. Much of what he decided to do, he said, was what the franchiser had suggested all along.

One thing he decided to do was to solve a recurring problem with inventory by installing a simple accumulation plan for parts which always had run out during his peak season. Another was to install a profit-sharing plan so employees had vested rights and retirement benefits. Another was to develop his accounting system for better planning and control.

Ken got so well organized that he considered expansion to a second location. His systems made such a move relatively simple, since he had trained personnel and controls which did not require his personal supervision. Ken took a real estate course, among others, to give himself more information about where to locate the new shop.

Finally, he dropped the franchise arrangement and purchased his own mufflers. This small business clearly moved into the administrative type of operation, and it continues to prosper and expand. Although many craft firms are small, there is no relationship between size and organization type. Ken Homes' firm is an example of an administrative type which is relatively small.

Definition of Good
It should be clear from the preceding discussion that no one stage is automatically "good" since "good" depends upon how one defines it. If good means comfort and survival, *not* growth, for a firm which has a stable niche in its market, the craft type may be good. For a leader who defines good as maximum growth to exploit a definite innovation, good may mean the promotion stage. Or, where good means long-run profitable operations with relatively little danger from competition, the administrative type may be best.

Thus, folklore like "a good company is a growing company," or "a firm has to grow, or it dies" may be misleading. If such statements were preceded by the words, "I believe that . . ." they would be better. As general rules, they have no basis in fact.

Summary and Preview
To summarize, in the last three chapters I have described three quite different types of organization. They are described as if one may find a single organization with all of the characteristics of a craft, promotion, or administrative type. In reality, each organization has some characteristics of all three types. This is not necessarily desirable. Once the types are clear, an executive can decide which type is best for her purposes and then move intentionally in the desired direction.

After a discussion in the next chapter of the leaders in each type, the remainder of this book will concentrate on how to achieve the administrative type or, if there, how to perform more effectively. Except under the special conditions described, most managers will find the administrative type to be of the greatest lasting benefit.

Chapter 6 Leadership

Cusins: *How do you maintain discipline among your men?*
Undershaft: *I don't. They do. Every man of them keeps the man just below him in his place. The men snub the boys and order them about; the carmen snub the sweepers; the artisans snub the unskilled laborers; the foremen drive and bully both the laborers and artisans; the assistant engineers find fault with the foremen; the chief engineers drop on the assistants; the departmental managers worry the chiefs; and the clerks have tall hats and hymnbooks and keep up the social tone by refusing to associate on equal terms with anybody.*

G. B. Shaw, *Major Barbara*

Focus on Behavior, not Traits

It is common practice in college education to ask students to write papers about subjects of personal interest. The process gives students an opportunity to dig more deeply into such topics, gives them practice in doing secondary research, and provides a further, often enjoyable, basis for student evaluation. When I teach a course related to the subject, it is not unusual for a student to say, "Professor Filley, I'd like to write a paper on leadership." I generally say, "What aspect or type of leadership?" The student may say, "Oh, I don't know, just leadership." If I say, "OK, go ahead," I can predict what will follow.

He will appear later to tell me that there is just too much written on leadership or that most of the literature doesn't make any sense scientifically. Then we get down to work, eliminating the popular literature which contains opinions rather than facts, narrowing the topic to something manageable.

Perhaps no subject in the field of management has so much written about it with so little meaning. Research and theory are supposed to lead to the eventual objective of explanation and prediction. Yet articles and books on leadership persist in presenting a list of traits which are supposed to characterize a successful leader: honesty, reverence, diligence . . . whatever. Such approaches are vacuous since the list of traits may be shown to be present in unsuccessful leaders as well. In contrast, the better studies which *do* provide explanation and prediction are likely to focus upon successful and unsuccessful leader *behavior* in different situations.

In this chapter I'd like to describe some of the leader behavior which does have a positive effect on people's performance and satisfaction. I'll also indicate how we can assess our own behavior in this regard and how you as a manager can improve your leadership skills.

The Craft Leader

Both the leader in the craft type of organization and the leader in the promotion type have particular characteristics which shape the nature of the organization. Many of these reflect the personality of the craftsman or the promoter. In the administrative type, however, leadership is much more a set of learned skills and is less dependent upon personality.

The top leaders in craft organizations will generally have started or entered the business after having worked in a technical specialty. A builder of machine tools for someone else may decide to start his own business. A design engineer may start her own engineering business. A musician may start his own music shop. While such people are in a position of leadership, they may not perform the actions of the administrative type, which I will describe later.

Craft leaders spend much of their time doing work that is similar to that performed by other people in the organization. Like Ken Homes installing mufflers with his helper, craftsmen work with others, building machine tools, selling, making engineering designs, or whatever the technology of the business happens to be. As a result, little time can be spent on the management work that has to be done, and no attempt is made to develop the skills associated with leadership of the administrative type.

This problem is not limited to craft leaders, either. In general, to the extent that managers, foremen, and supervisors spend time doing work that is like that of their subordinates, they are less likely to be effective as leaders. Such action merely reduces the time available for planning, improving methods, training, or the other duties of a manager.

Craft leaders seem to prefer a stable, secure enterprise which does not grow. For example, a home builder in Chicago said to me, "Look, Filley, I have discovered that I'm not a good manager. I can eyeball two construction jobs at one time, but more than that and I have to rely on others to supervise the projects. When I do that, things get fouled up. Anyway, I'm making more money than I need, and I'm happy with my life." Would you argue with that? I wouldn't. Management folklore says that "a good business is a growing business," but in the case of the craft organization, the most sensible strategy may well be to limit the size of the firm if it can continue to operate at a profit with less danger to its survival.

Finally, as suggested in Chapter 3, craft leaders place much emphasis on experience. They feel that one can't learn how to run her business from books or training programs. To a certain extent they are right. The predictors of business success suggest that one ought to have training *and* experience. Training provides resources, alternatives, and ways to improve decision making. Experience provides wisdom and good sense. I wouldn't argue with the craftsman's belief in the value of experience, only with his belief that a person who hasn't worked in his business can't tell him how to do the job better.

The Promoter
In contrast with the craftsman, the promoter displays a great deal of risk-taking behavior. He appears to be high in a personality characteristic called need for achievement. People with a high need for achievement have some rather clear patterns of behavior. They take moderate risks; that is, they are not interested in bad gambles and they are not interested in perfectly safe actions either. They have high standards of performance, often taking personal responsibility for what goes on. They need regular feedback on their accomplishments, perhaps explaining why promoters like to see rapid sales increases.[1] They also seem to be able to work effectively under unstructured, ambiguous situations.[2]

While people in other organization types also may be high in the need for achievement, it is easy to see why this characteristic would aid the promoter. Starting a new enterprise to exploit an untested product is certainly risky. In addition, with no track record, the production and marketing of the product require decision making under ambiguous conditions.

Perhaps this need for achievement may account for promoters often saying they are not in business for the money—the dollars are just a way to keep score. The promoter's need for personal responsibility may also explain why he tries to run everything. While there may be a minimal organizational structure, the promoter gives directions to and has personal contact with most people in the organization.

Promoters typically have difficulty in dealing with authority. They have trouble taking orders from others and give orders to subordinates in a very personal way. This behavior pattern has been explained in a study of entrepreneurs, *The Enterprising Man*.[3] According to the authors of that study, the promoter typically grows up in a situation in which the role of a father is either minimal or absent. Since we learn how to deal with authority at an early age through our father (or father substitute), the promoter never develops that capacity.

According to the study, the promoter also lives on his own initiative at a relatively early age. He starts his own enterprises or moves from job to job, showing an unusual tolerance for failure and often experiencing conflict with superiors. Starting or running his own enterprise gives him an opportunity to be free of the authority of others and to meet his needs for achievement.

The least explainable characteristic of the promoter is his charisma in the eyes of subordinates. He is a hero. He is endowed in their eyes with exceptional powers. I see this phenomenon repeatedly in promotion firms. When I interview employees of this and other types of organizations, one of my standard questions is: "Why did you come to work at this company?" The usual response in promotion firms is: "I talked with Mr. So-and-So, and I *knew* that this was the place for me." In administrative firms the response is more likely to be: "Because this was the best job I looked at." In the latter case, the employee's boss is his foreman or supervisor or manager. In the promotion firm, the boss is clearly the promoter.

Maybe the promoter gets his charisma because of his success, or maybe he gets it just because he attracts people who want a hero—I don't know. But I do know that being a charismatic leader is both a blessing and a curse. It is a blessing because charismatic leaders motivate people to extremes of effort.

In the movie, "Lawrence of Arabia,"[4] there is a scene that illustrates this influence. Lawrence wanted to cross the desert to the sea, and one of the native leaders said it couldn't be done. Lawrence wanted to know why. The native said something like: "Because it is written" (traditional policy). Lawrence replied that *nothing* is written and crossed the desert.

Another standard question that I ask is: "What are the costs of working here? What do you give up that you would have if you worked for another company?" A frequent response in promotional firms is: "Well, I don't get to spend enough time with my family." Rarely do people talk about their wages, the extra hours that they work, or the crowded, confused working conditions.

The curse of the charismatic leader is the crucifixion syndrome. This is my label for the fact that when people put a leader on a pedestal, they invariably end up knocking her off the pedestal. To explain this, my guess is that charismatic leaders, being perceived as perfect, aren't allowed to make mistakes. Since it is impossible to avoid failure all the time, heroes do fail, and when they do, their followers show great disappointment and anger. I have already mentioned in Chapter 4 that the later part of the promotion firm's existence is often accompanied by turnover of long-service people, disenchantment with the leader, and unionizing attempts. I wish I had a solution for this problem, but it may be some satisfaction to promoters who have had this experience to know that the problem is common, not unique to them.

The promoter's role is particularly useful in dealing with the change and ambiguity associated with handling an innovation in a rapidly growing enterprise. The leader holds things together in the confusion of the promotion firm. There is no great need for efficiency since the profit margins permit costly operation, but there is a need for decision making and direction, and this the promoter can effectively provide. Once things change to a situation demanding structure and efficiency, the promoter's decision-making ability loses its advantage and such a leadership style may create serious problems. Promoters may continue to be comfortable without much structure, even though subordinates feel a need for predictability and greater freedom in their jobs.

Both the leader of the promotion type of organization

and the leader of the craft type have a major impact upon their firms. I have seen this happen in businesses with 5 or 6 employees as well as those with 500 employees. The impact of one person is substantially less in the administrative type of organization since it is an institution which often has many leaders who have influence, each with her own subordinates.

Behavior of the Administrative Leader
When I speak of leadership, I mean basically the ability of an *individual* to establish and maintain acceptable levels of satisfaction and job-related performance so that *organization* needs are met as well. This is probably more difficult in the administrative type of organization than it is in the other two for lots of reasons. Perhaps the most important of these is the fact that individuals in administrative organizations are more likely to make job comparisons with other organizations. Salesperson X says, "Do I get a better deal with this company than I could with another?" In contrast, the people in the middle and upper levels of the craft firm are so locked into the organization that they are less likely to conceive of working elsewhere, and people in the promotion firm are so enthusiastic about the future that they don't think about alternatives.

Because employees in the administrative type are willing to leave it if things aren't OK and because of the needs for efficiency in the administrative organization, the task of leadership in this type requires greater performance capabilities. At a general level of thinking, performance depends on ability and motivation, and ability depends on aptitude, experience, and training. Obviously, the kind and degree of aptitude or experience or training required will vary from task to task and from job to job. There is no reason to believe that a leader in one organization who is successful will also be successful in another organization unless the circumstances are quite similar.

As leaders, you and I deal with three essential elements. The first is *people.* We select them, train them, motivate them, and provide a means for them to work together. The second is *organization*. We provide systems and controls within which people operate. The third is *resources*. We provide things like money and raw materials and, importantly, information. There are trade-offs between these three related areas. For example, like the traffic light in Chapter 2, effective organization can reduce the amount of information processing required (by indicating that red means stop) and can provide a means for people to coordinate their actions.

The trade-offs involved between people, organization, and resources are illustrated in the experience of a client of mine. The company makes a component for the electronics industry and has evolved in recent years from a promotion organization to an administrative type. Its product has been mass-produced for some years in other companies, but this firm specializes in a segment of the market which demands highly reliable, special-purpose items, and its customers have been willing to pay a premium for the product. The company had about 300 employees when I first had contact with it and had grown rapidly to that point.

The president was clearly charismatic to his employees. He is tall, slim, sleeps four hours a night, is highly intelligent, and is intense in his behavior. He and a personal assistant exerted pervasive influence upon all operations in the company. When I first had contact with it, the company had minimal formal systems. In fact, the president insisted that the company would continue with that form, and he would not utilize job titles, job descriptions, written policies, or clear separation of departmental duties. When I interviewed the managers and supervisors in the company, it became apparent that one of the norms in the firm was antipathy against any type of conventional method. In other words, it was believed that, "If it has been done before, it's bad."

The degree of information processing in the organization placed enormous demands upon the president and the managers. They worked more than one shift and often part of the weekend to keep up with the pressure. One of my objectives was to clarify the fact that if supporting systems which provided efficiency and reliability could be standardized, resources would be freed for those areas which demanded creativity and adaptability. Having an unconventional personnel system or budget system or purchasing system merely drained off time and energy that could be better spent upon product design, research, sales, and customer service.

Eventually, whether due to my influence or not, the company changed its type to an administrative form. Planning, budgeting, scheduling, stated policies, utilization of middle managers, and formalization have all taken place. The firm is institutionalized now with a secure position in its industry. The organization now provides a set of standing orders (traffic lights) which reduces the amount of personal supervision necessary, increases the ease of achieving coordinated action, and reduces the amount of information processing required.

The leadership in this company has changed too. While the president is still energetic and personally impressive, it is not likely that company success depends entirely upon him. He has a team of executives and middle managers who lead their own subordinates.

Leader Behavior under Different Conditions
The folklore of management contains much advice. It tells us: "Nice guys don't win (they finish last)," and "If you get too close to people, they take advantage of you." Folklore also says, "Most people want to be told what to do; they can't think for themselves," and "Happy people are productive." Little wonder that people are confused.

Fortunately, the research on leader behavior is beginning to show some patterns. The research on this subject indicates that the type of leadership which is most effective depends greatly on the particular situation. Fortunately, as well, these patterns give us a pretty good idea of what works when.

Two convergent streams of research are particularly helpful here. The first is work done at Ohio State University since 1947[5] which has identified two key components of leadership behavior. The second is provided by Robert J. House,[6] who has identified different kinds of leader behavior required in different situations.

Research on Leadership

The Ohio State studies began with an attempt to describe *behaviors* which leaders exhibit when they lead. Instead of focusing upon traits such as the leader's appearance, intelligence, personality, and the like, the Ohio State group considered actions taken, such as setting job standards or consulting with subordinates. Their efforts resulted in two clusters of behaviors which seem to be present in all kinds of leaders. The first of these clusters contains behaviors which are social in nature: treating subordinates as equals, being accessible to subordinates, explaining actions taken, being responsive to suggestions, and representing the needs of subordinates to others. These and other similar behaviors formed a cluster which they identified as "consideration." The second cluster contains behaviors which have to do with structuring the work or with pressure for high levels of job performance: scheduling work to be done, making job assignments, insisting upon work at full capacity, and criticizing poor work. These and other similar statements formed a cluster which they labeled "initiating structure."* (Throughout this chapter and in some other parts of the book the terms consideration and initiating structure will be used in this sense designated by the Ohio State group.)

Since these clusters are independent of each other, it might be possible for a leader to be high on consideration and

---

*The Ohio State questionnaire which describes the degree to which an individual is exhibiting each set of behaviors is known as *The Leader Behavior Description Questionnaire* (Form XII). It may be completed by the leader's superior, by the leader himself, or by several subordinates. The latter is generally preferred, since the results are more reliable. The instrument may be used to answer several kinds of questions: Has our training program actually changed leader behavior? What is the relative difference among our managers on consideration and initiating structure? How do the levels of consideration and initiating structure of our managers compare with those in managers of similar organizations?

low on initiating structure, low on consideration and high on initiating structure, or high or low on both. Both consideration and initiating structure have been separately recommended as ideal approaches to leadership. In the 1930s and 1940s, the recommended approach was one of good human relations, which is similar to what is here called consideration. Quite correctly, experienced managers probably read the literature on leadership at that time and got the feeling that if they practiced what was recommended, they were in danger of giving away the store. Human relations proponents seemed to ignore emphasis on getting work accomplished.

On the other hand, writers in the early part of this century stressed that a good leader was demanding and highly organized, characteristics not unlike those of initiating structure. Again, the experienced manager probably felt that the recommendations were too simple and that to be a tough manager invited hostility from those supervised. In fact, both the human relations approach and the demanding, organized approach worked part of the time and failed part of the time. General rules seldom work all the time. The trick, it seems, is to figure out what works when.

The Ohio State group helped to improve an understanding of leadership by demonstrating that satisfied and productive work groups were frequently led by leaders who were described by their subordinates as high in *both* consideration and initiating structure behavior. They demonstrated that it is possible to be demanding and also to be sensitive to the needs of people supervised. However, as the research findings about the two dimensions of leadership were reported, it became clear that they contained some contradictory results.

The next pieces in the puzzle of what works when and the answer to early contradictory findings were added by Robert J. House when he presented two basic ideas stemming from his own study of leader behavior. His first idea is that a leader's behavior will be accepted by subordinates and will be satisfying to them when they see such behavior as either a source of immediate satisfaction or as an aid to gaining future satisfaction. In other words, you are pleased with your leader to the extent that she meets your present needs—say, for recognition—or provides a way to meet your needs in the future—say, to gain a promotion.

House's second basic idea is that a leader's behavior will motivate subordinates—increase their work effort—if gaining satisfaction depends upon doing a good job and if the leader's behavior provides them with resources necessary for doing a good job. In other words, you are likely to work more effectively if the leader rewards you for doing a good job and if your leader fills in things that you need to do a good job: increases your skill through training, gives you guidance when that job is not clear to you, or shows you how to get more future satisfaction.

These pieces of the puzzle, that is, the identification of behavior associated with consideration and initiating structure, plus the identification of conditions under which those behaviors make people satisfied or productive, have provided the answers to many questions about leadership. They are not the whole picture, to be sure, but they do explain how to improve leadership and suggest ideas which make sense and have real support.

Application of Findings

Suggested Rules
An employee's satisfaction with his boss depends upon the degree of consideration displayed by the boss. In many different organizations and at all organizational levels there is consistent support for the idea that satisfaction with a superior is closely related to the social skill, or consideration, of the leader. In other words, if you want to be liked by subordinates, exercise high levels of consideration. This in no way predicts subordinate performance levels, however.

Consideration by a leader will have more effect on subordinate satisfaction where the work is unpleasant and stressful than it will where work is pleasant and unstressful. In other words, where the work is satisfying in the first place, consideration will have less impact than where it is not satisfying work. Where conditions are stressful, leaders should be high in consideration behavior.

If a leader is high in consideration, he can exercise more initiating structure without reducing subordinate satisfaction. This finding resolves the tough guy versus nice guy dilemma which has existed for many years. It demonstrates that in practicing good human relations, a manager creates the right to also expect and require high levels of subordinate performance. If you like your boss and he is considerate of your needs, you will accept the fact that he sets high standards of performance. If your boss is not considerate and expects high levels of performance, you may become angry or resistant.

Consideration by the boss will affect subordinate performance when it is given for successful job performance. When a leader pays attention to, is influenced by, or is supportive of good job performers—not poor job performers—she will increase the likelihood of good job performance. The opposite is illustrated when a leader takes the time to listen to dirty jokes from an employee. Since listening to someone is a reward in itself, the leader is training the subordinate to tell dirty jokes, not to produce. When consideration behaviors are not given differently to high and low performers, such behavior may have no effect on productivity.

Initiating structure by a leader will increase the satisfaction of subordinates when it adds clarity to an ambiguous situation. For example, committee members will be pleased when the chair of a committee says, "Ladies and gentlemen, we will be meeting for one hour to deal with each of the items stated on this agenda." On the other hand, they may not be pleased when the chair says, "Well, folks, let's meet until we are finished and talk about some things on my mind and whatever you want to talk about."

Similarly, employees are also pleased when the leader says, "Here is a new task that you have never done before. Let me show you how to do it." When the leader *fills in* structure that is missing, employees are likely to be satisfied.

Initiating structure will decrease satisfaction where structure is already present. Where job methods are clear and the standards for reward are known, a leader who adds even more structure may merely cause frustration and dissatisfaction. For example, employees doing work on a production line where the work is already paced and structured will probably resist a foreman who tries to give advice and assistance that they feel is unnecessary. For such jobs, the foreman should probably be high in consideration and he should reserve attempts to structure to new employees—or be prepared to answer questions that come up.

Initiating structure by a leader will increase productivity when the task is not clear. To the extent that a boss can reduce sources of confusion, make work easier, define priorities, or show connections between work methods and rewards, he is likely to elicit better job performance from his subordinates.

Initiating structure by a leader will not affect performance where the task is clear. Obviously, if you already know how to perform the job and how to get the rewards you need, then such structure does not add anything to your performance. The opposite is illustrated in the experience of the president of a company manufacturing a medical product. With relatively uneducated, marginal employees, this company makes a product that is ordinarily produced by highly skilled technicians. The company is located in a large urban center and employs individuals who often have only done the most menial kind of work.

The president has divided the manufacturing steps into small segments, has defined the performance standards in each segment, and has trained new employees in the performance of their jobs. The result is high productivity and technical proficiency with minimally skilled new employees.

On the basis of the previous discussion, if you want to have satisfied subordinates you should:

- Achieve a high level of social skill.

- Provide a high level of social support where the work is stressful or unpleasant.

- Take care to structure work where the task is ambiguous to subordinates.

- Overcome obstacles to achievement of job rewards by subordinates (clarify rules, train, protect from outside interference, provide necessary resources).

- Avoid giving detailed instruction on job methods to subordinates who already know how to do the task.

- Avoid demanding high performance from people who already display high performance patterns of behavior.

On the basis of what has been said, if you want productive subordinates you should:

- Give social support to good producers, but not to poor producers.

- Provide a high level of social support *and* structure ambiguous tasks (clarify rules, train, protect from outside interference, provide necessary resources, set performance standards, schedule work, set priorities).

- Provide a high level of social support *and* demand high performance where high performance patterns are not present.

There are other elements in the job of leadership, but the task and social behaviors in initiating structure and consideration are fairly well understood and are clearly documented. As a general objective, most of us would do well to try for a high level of proficiency in both of these dimensions. To start a self-improvement program, you should determine which of these represents your strength and which your weakness. It's unlikely that people will be high in both without some development effort.

Development of Skills
The *development* of skills in the task and social areas requires two entirely different approaches, however. Task skills, or initiating structure, requires an intellectual learning process and then practice. Most of this book is devoted to methods of management which will improve task skills. In addition, you might want to observe successful managers in action,

attend education or training programs, and develop a regular reading program on task-related matters. Many task skills are learned in the same way one learns to use an adding machine, prepare an income statement, or read a road map. The obstacle to developing task skills is much more likely to be motivation than ability.

In contrast, developing social skills, or consideration, depends heavily upon experiences of deep emotional involvement with people. I doubt whether social skills are enhanced much by reading books like *The Power of Positive Thinking*[7] or *How to Win Friends and Influence People*,[8] or whatever today's version might be. Social skills grow out of positive feelings about oneself and about others and, importantly, from an absence of threat or defensiveness. In extreme cases, such development may be enhanced by therapy. I wouldn't knock it. For other cases, I'd suggest sensitivity training or encounter groups.

I do not wish to say much about such groups here. If you are interested in the subject, write me a letter for information; contact legitimate centers such as the National Training Laboratories in Washington, D.C., or the Esalen Institute in Big Sur, California, or one listed in your local area; or ask your minister, personnel manager, or a local college faculty member to recommend one. Since the best predictor of future behavior is past behavior, it is important to check out the trainer and training institution by talking to people who have attended the encounter groups in question or who know the qualifications of the trainer.

Such encounter groups became very faddish in the 1960s and, as might be expected, the whole thing became distorted with some weird trainers and by some extremists. I have been associated with dozens of such groups over the last ten years and I have *never* observed a group which: (a) was a sexual orgy, (b) was conducted in the nude, (c) spent its time tearing up the members, (d) was a Communist conspiracy, or (e) brainwashed its participants. Not everyone benefits, but the result often is enhanced social skills and a profound appreciation of each person's unique gifts.*

Other Facets of Leadership

In addition to task and social skills, there are a number of other facets of leader behavior which appear to be associated with job success. Leaders who are successful display technical knowledge about the area for which they are responsible. Technical knowledge is reflected in the leader's ability to give sensible orders and to differentiate between good and bad performance. The leader doesn't have to be able to do the subordinate's job as well as the subordinate can, but the leader must be able to give specific and appropriate job objectives. In addition, unless the leader can tell the difference between good and bad performance, rewards cannot be allocated for performance, and subordinates will be *trained by the leader* to be inefficient and unproductive.

Successful leaders display decision-making processes that are appropriate in different situations. They know when to call a meeting, when to turn a decision over to someone else, when to shoot from the hip, when to announce a decision and enforce it. However, it is not uncommon for the leader in a one-man-show kind of growing organization to eventually become the greatest single obstacle to the success of the organization. No matter how bright, energetic, or knowledgeable the one-man-show leader is, he can become the key bottleneck to information processing in the organization because he fails to utilize others in decision making.

Successful leaders are generally relatively well informed about what is happening outside the organization. Through their reading efforts, involvement in community affairs, and contact with others in their profession, they seem to be more adaptive and creative. One leader may have read *The Joy of*

---

*For the record, I'm uncomfortable around people who have picked up the jargon of encounter groups without learning their real lessons. Such people say, "Let me *share* this with you," or "I feel that you aren't *leveling* with me," or "I want to be open and honest with you." They also act as if people who haven't attended an encounter group are uninitiated and outsiders.

Sex and another may have read a history of England. The imagery the two use may differ somewhat, but both are likely to be more creative compared with someone who has read nothing.

Successful leaders generally display a sense of futurity in their behavior. They have a picture in their minds of an ideal future and direct the efforts of themselves and others toward specific goals to achieve it. In contrast, if leaders only maintain the status quo and have no sense of futurity, the organization can be vulnerable and nonadaptive.

Finally, successful leaders generally display a level of health and energy that is commensurate with job demands. The human body experiences some changes somewhere around the age of forty which can result in mental and emotional deterioration. Facility in these areas can be maintained through health-supporting activities like exercise, or it can be allowed to wane. For this reason, active exercise programs like swimming, jogging, tennis, or handball are good signs.

Summary and Preview

The various facets of leader behavior which have been discussed here are generally associated with effectiveness. While there are exceptions to these facets and while other elements also play a part in leader success, the behaviors mentioned provide some specific goals for a person wishing to improve ability as a leader. They also should be useful in improving the odds of employing a person in a leadership position who is likely to be successful. In the next chapter, I'll be adding further information about leader behavior when I discuss motivation of subordinates.

Chapter 7   Motivation of Others

When men have to do with one another, they are like verbs— almost all verbs are irregular.

Soren Kirkegaard

Seeking Satisfaction
In my association with business people and managers of social or government agencies I am often asked, "Why aren't people motivated anymore? No one wants to work. What are you teaching these kids when they are in school? Is it the way they were raised—permissiveness and all that? Is society changing?" When I ask for an example, the manager may say, "Well, I have this guy working for me who does just enough to avoid being fired. He comes in late at least once a week He doesn't meet production schedules. And, he is the first one to leave in the evening. I guess he's just lazy—he sure isn't motivated like some others I've seen."

If we pursue the subject and find out what the subordinate does on and off the job, we are likely to find that he is actively engaged in something during most of his waking hours. During the workday he talks with others, makes work assignments, reviews progress of production, handles emergencies, makes and receives phone calls, and attends formal meetings. When he leaves the job, he mows the lawn, washes the car, plays football with his kids, repairs his house, and watches television. In short, he is nearly always busy.

We are all motivated in that sense. We are actively doing something which we somehow feel to be rewarding or something which we feel will avoid some kind of cost. Employees who are judged to be unmotivated or unproductive are only unmotivated or unproductive in the sense that what they are doing does not contribute to what the employer feels will meet his needs or those of the organization. In a way, the unproductive employee simply feels that she can get a "better deal" utilizing activity in some way other than meeting the goals of the organization.

A lot of explanations have been offered to clarify how we calculate the best deal from among our choices for action. The simplest, hedonism, says that we seek pleasure and avoid pain. An extended version of this, the Law of Effect, says that, given a variety of choices for action, we will select the one that we have found to be most satisfying and avoid those that have been experienced as dissatisfying. Left at that, though, human beings would be pretty passive agents. What they do would depend upon their experience—the associations they have made in the past between actions and outcomes. Yet common sense tells us that people set goals for themselves which are not based upon past experience.

The thing that we seek has been loosely and imperfectly described as satisfaction (or avoidance of dissatisfaction). It is well to remember that satisfaction is an abstraction like wealth, or economics, or living creatures. In fact, the satisfaction that people seek includes a variety of things: consistency between values and actions, pleasant sensations, absence from guilt, victory, a sense of fairness, peace of mind, satiation of needs, or simply stimulation. Some actions are directed to needs we are born with—hunger, sex, thirst. Some are affected by definitions of good or bad that we acquire— "masturbation is evil." Some we develop through experience—movies are entertaining. Others we develop through expectations about the future—college will be interesting. All these and more fall under the general heading of satisfaction.

Given the previous explanation, I'd like to summarize and say that people do those things which they *think* will lead to satisfaction and avoid those things which they *think* will reduce satisfaction or create dissatisfaction. We do not *want* to be productive or to serve an organization; instead we actively seek to acquire personal gains or to avoid personal costs, and these gains or costs we loosely identify as satisfaction or dissatisfaction. Such actions on our part, if they contribute to organizational goals, cause us to be judged as productive by people who care about such things.

Process Instead of Content
As with the subject of leadership, the literature and teaching on motivation have not been much help in the past. Happily, there are now some facts which help us to understand the process of motivation and help us to improve the motivation of others toward goals which the manager or organization defines as productive. As with leadership, the useful information with tool value comes more from understanding the *process* rather than the *content* of motivation. Content theories of motivation have presented lists of needs—for recognition,

social acceptance, achievement, self-actualization, and the like. Process approaches to the subject focus instead on the calculations and behaviors which you or I go through in deciding where to direct our actions. While the content theories, like Herzberg's[1] mentioned in Chapter 5, have provided some useful information about the kinds of things that people like, they have not been entirely useful when applied to the motivation of individuals.

As a first step in considering the realities of the subject, let's explore a bit of folklore. We have been told, "Happy people are productive." Obviously, some are and some aren't. As with the leader high in consideration behavior who is likely to influence satisfaction, happiness in no way guarantees good performance. In fact, the most accurate and well-documented statement which one can make about satisfaction as a cause of behavior is that people satisfied with their employment are more likely to come to work and stay at work than people dissatisfied with it. In other words, turnover and absenteeism rates are generally higher for dissatisfied employees than for satisfied employees.

This may not seem like much, but I'll show why it has great tool value to a manager. Getting a fact—a real fact—that holds up across lots of situations is like getting a saw after you have been cutting trees with an axe all your life. A fact is a tool. To demonstrate its usefulness, let me recall a common experience of mine. I occasionally meet an employer who has just conducted a morale survey with his employees. He has obtained a survey form from his trade association, out of a book, or from a friend. The form generally asks the person completing it to place a check mark on a scale next to some facet of employment, indicating her degree of satisfaction or dissatisfaction. For example, on the facet of pay, the form might look like this:

Indicate your degree
of satisfaction with:

                                                     X

Your pay   Dissatisfied 1 2 3 4 5 6 7 Satisfied

This seems to indicate that the employee is mildly dissatisfied with pay. She also is asked to rate other facets such as supervision, the company, her job, opportunities for promotion, and the like.

After the survey is complete, the employer may say to me, "Filley, we have just completed a morale survey, and I want you to look over the results. The company average was five. What does that mean?" I say, "I don't know, do you?" He says, "No, I don't, that's why I'm asking you. Five looks pretty good, though, doesn't it?" I say, "Well, it's bigger than four all right. But, what would the number have been a year ago—seven? Two? And, what would it be for other firms in town?"

He says, "Then the whole thing was a waste of time?" I say, "No, there are a lot of useful comparisons that you can make, and the first is based on the fact that happy people come to work and stay at work more than unhappy ones. The big question is *whether your happy people are your top producers or your worst producers.*"

We then proceed to break down the people responding into the good guys and the bad guys. For our purpose the good guys may be defined by scores on company merit rating forms, production records or supervisor rankings based on performance. When this is done, we look at the result of the merit rating for each group. After determining whether the difference in scores is real or just based on random fluctuations from the measurement procedure, we can tell whether the good guys are more satisfied than the bad guys. For example, if the average for the good guys is six and for the bad guys three, we know that the people whom we are most likely to lose are the poor producers. If, on the other hand, the score for the good guys is lower than the score for the bad guys, we know that the chances for losing our top producers are greater than for losing our low producers.

This procedure does not give us information about the survey results compared with other places of employment, company history, or universal standards. It might provide a way to improve satisfaction of poor producers, however, if obvious sources of dissatisfaction are indicated. In some cases the employer may simply count his blessings and avoid tinkering with anything. He would make a mistake, however, if he tried to improve performance by dealing with the things that the employees are not happy about. Only if more satisfaction is gained through better performance would such efforts be appropriate.

Review and Application of Research
To increase individual performance, the employer might well start by considering the process that people utilize when they choose where to direct their efforts. For the sake of illustration, we'll assume that the choice is to direct effort at a high or low level of output. The same logic applies, however, in any question of choosing to do something: going to college, choosing between two employers, going to a party, taking up golf. Each is the motivation to do something. The major contributors to the understanding of this process are Edward Lawler[2] at the University of Michigan and Victor Vroom[3] at Yale University. They suggest that in choosing to exert effort or to be motivated to high or low levels of performance, each individual makes a series of judgments or estimates. Paraphrasing their work, we can consider the following key questions the individual asks:

1. What is the likelihood that if I try to achieve high (or low) performance, I can do it?

2. As I see the results (both positive and negative) from high (or low) performance, what is the likelihood that they will happen?

3. How valuable or desirable are the outcomes which I expect to get from high (or low) performance?

These estimates are considered to be multiplied times each other. The reason is simple: just as 1000 times zero is zero, if the answer to any of the questions is zero, motivation is zero. If I don't believe that I can do what is expected, I won't try. If I believe that the outcomes of high performance, such as more money, are desirable but unlikely, while the outcomes of lower performance, like being employed, are guaranteed, then I won't try for higher performance. Finally, if I don't like the rewards I get with higher performance, then I won't try.

In the following discussion about the motivation process we will add another question which has an important effect on motivation:

4. What, exactly, is the definition of high (or low) performance expected?

The reason for this question will be apparent shortly.

Considering each of these four questions (although not in the preceding order), we can get some rather simple and straightforward tools for enhancing employee motivation.

What is the likelihood that if I try to achieve high (or low) performance, I can do it? One element in the process which leads to effort to produce (motivation) is the estimate which each individual makes about his relative ability to do what is involved. This estimate is somewhere between 100 percent certainty that he can perform and a belief that he can't do it at all. It must be emphasized that regardless of how facts enter the picture, the determining factor is a personal opinion about ability to perform. A person's "reality" depends on how he perceives the given situation.

A variety of things probably influences this estimate. One is the objective situation. If my task is to type a letter and I have no typewriter, my estimate of performing is zero. Another is my perception of my ability. If high performance means giving a speech and I expect that I'd be too nervous to do it, then my perceptions reduce my estimate of ability to perform. A third influence is information that I get from others. If my foreman can demonstrate to me that I can perform at the high level required, the question is no longer whether I *can* do the job, only whether I *want* to do it.

A direct application of this approach used recently in industry is entry training for marginal workers. Individuals who have never held continuous employment in any but the most menial kind of work are shown how to get to the place of employment and how to perform the required work in a simulated job setting. They are shown that the effort and skill required are possible for them if they want to perform.

Another influence on a person's estimate of the ability to do a job is experience in the present or similar job situations. If I have performed at a required level in other situations, or to the extent that I am repeatedly successful in the present one, my estimates about being able to perform increase. Finally, self-image, or self-esteem, plays a part. If I feel that I am a loser and can't do anything right, my estimates in the immediate situation will be low. Because of this, if management lowers the self-esteem of employees, it merely causes less motivation on the part of employees.

Eric Berne put this nicely when he said, "We are all born princes and princesses, but our Parents turn us into Frogs."[4] In his language, Parents are people who can affect our self-esteem and Frogs are losers.

Based on this information, if you want to enhance motivation, you can:

• Demonstrate to each employee that high-level job performance is possible.

• Increase self-esteem among present employees.

• Employ people with high self-esteem.

• Change job designs so that people can succeed within their objective capabilities.

• Transfer employees to jobs in which they can succeed.

What, exactly, is the definition of a high (or low) performance expected? In other words, how clearly is the job defined? I find, and the evidence clearly supports my experience, that managers generally do a terrible job of making job assignments. Curiously, when they contract services outside their firm, they are often much more specific than when they make equally important job assignments within the organization. For example, a manager contracting to have a new parking lot installed will likely agree with the contractor on the cost, time, materials, color, durability, manpower, and guarantees about exceptions. This same manager, when assigning a project to a subordinate, may say only, "Do a good job."

In a workshop I attended, George Odiorne of the University of Massachusetts reported that he has surveyed large numbers of manager-subordinate combinations, asking the manager what his subordinate's job is as he (the manager) would like to see it accomplished and asking the subordinate what his job is as the manager would like to see it accomplished. In other words, the subordinate's job is described by the manager and by the subordinate as he thinks the manager wants it. The result, says Odiorne, is that the two descriptions vary by about 25 percent.

This result explains a variety of phenomena. For one thing, it suggests why so many managers complain that they can't find good subordinates and that no one seems to want to work much anymore. It also explains why subordinates often say they are never able to please the boss. They say, "He always tells me about things I do wrong, but I never get a compliment." Much inadequate performance, it seems, occurs because managers create it!

In some related research, Ed Locke and associates[5] at the University of Maryland have experimented with pairs of similar groups, giving each the same task to do. One group was told "Do your best." The other group was given a specific goal like: make twenty-five in one hour. Locke et al. have shown that as long as the people in the specific-goal group accept the goal and believe that it can be accomplished, they generally outperform the group told to do their best.

Similarly, in experimenting with tight and loose time standards, Locke et al. demonstrated that the people in the tight-standard group outperform those in the other, providing again that they accept the goal.

Considering the work of both Odiorne and Locke et al., we can see that it seems likely that problems with motivation may be due to poor goal setting by a manager in the first place. One's boss is an important source of rewards, and it does not seem logical that subordinates intentionally try to avoid earning these rewards from him.

Based on this evidence, if you as employer want to enhance motivation, you should:

- Clearly identify the desired performance, providing clear goals, models of desired behavior, and written standards.
- Identify time limits for accomplishing job goals.
- Insure that goals are accepted by employees.

As I see the results (both positive and negative) from high (or low) performance, what is the likelihood that they will happen? This element in the motivation process involves my estimate of the likelihood that each performance will result in certain kinds of outcomes. For each outcome that I see as a possibility, I estimate the likelihood of the outcome occurring from complete assurance to no assurance. For example, at a high level of job performance the employee may see as possible: more income, increased chance for promotion, rejection by others as a "ratebuster," recognition by the boss, and a sense of achievement for himself. Conversely, in performing at a low level, the employee may see as possible outcomes: less income, no chance for promotion, acceptance by others, no recognition by the boss, and no sense of achievement for himself. In the case of *each outcome,* the employee will determine the likelihood of its occurrence if the specified performance takes place.

Suppose, for example, the boss says, "Yeah, Joe, we try to give pay increases and promotions to people who do a good job," and Joe's co-workers say, "Ratebusters are all lonely people around here." The likelihood of the former happiness may seem much less for Joe than the likelihood of the latter situation. In contrast, suppose the boss says, "Look, Joe, we have a piecework system here and for every unit produced we pay one dollar," and Joe's co-workers say nothing about rejecting high producers. Joe's estimates of outcome may be considerably different.

A number of things will affect these estimates. Again, the objective situation and the person's perceptions will be an influence. For example, there is a clear link between performance and outcome in piece-rate systems. In addition, the perceptions or experience of others will be a factor. If I am told, "Don't knock yourself out to get a promotion, the boss only promotes his relatives," my estimate of promotion outcomes may decrease even though the information may not be true. My experience in this or similar situations may be another factor. If I produce at a high level and get a sense of achievement, the odds of getting that sense again may increase.

Personality also plays a part. One personality factor is a person's sense of internal versus external control. People with high internal control characteristics believe that what happens to them is strongly influenced by their own efforts. People high in external control believe that what happens to them is largely controlled by fate or things beyond their own influence.

For example, if you are high in internal control and I say, "What is the likelihood that you will be accepted by a new group of people?" you may say, "Oh, pretty high. You see, what I do is introduce myself and learn the interests of the group members and ask them about things that I know they like to talk about." In contrast, if you are high in external control you may say, "Pretty low. It's chancy business. Some groups will accept you, and some won't. You just have to wait and find out." As might be expected, internal-control people will have higher estimates of their performance leading to outcomes than will external-control people.

Finally, as already implied, an organization and its management can do much to increase the odds of performance leading to outcomes through their policies and formal practices. Published pay systems, standards for promotion, clear policies, and formal performance evaluation can help in establishing perceived links between performance and rewards.

Based on the above discussion, if you want to increase motivation, you should:

- Clarify the links between performance and rewards.

- Give rewards for desired behavior and not for undesired behavior.

- Employ people with high internal control.

- Establish formal systems for achieving organization rewards.

How valuable or desirable are the outcomes which I expect to get from high (or low) performance? Each of the perceived results from my high performance, no matter how likely or unlikely its attainment, will have some kind of value to me, ranging from desirable to undesirable. That seems obvious enough. Yet what managers persist in ignoring is that different people want different things.

Let me illustrate. Recently I was consulting with a company that had a small shop for tool making. The shop had a new, young foreman, one older worker, and three young employees. The foreman had instituted his own incentive bonus by giving the week's top worker a six-pack of beer that he paid for himself. I happened to talk to the young employee who had won the beer the previous week. I said, "I hear you won the beer last week. That must have pleased you." "Yeah," he said, and frowned. I said, "You don't seem to be happy about it." He responded, "Why should I be? I don't drink beer. I wish the son of a gun had given me the money instead. I could have used that. *The foreman loves beer.* I hate the stuff!"

In other words, you and I persist in giving people rewards that are things we like instead of finding out what they like. I recall a homily that says: "We can control what people get, not what they want." To give people rewards that we value often results in no motivation on their part and perhaps a feeling on our part that the receivers are *ungrateful.* People do their own evaluation of the outcomes they receive or are likely to receive.

A number of things influence the way in which outcomes are valued. The order in which outcomes are received has some effect. People who are concerned with survival and safety may not value recognition and achievement and other higher needs until those for survival and safety are met. Another influence is the level to which certain needs are satisfied. Some needs, like thirst, are satisfied at some point. Other needs, like the realization of personal potential, seem not to be satisfied or satiated. The value of outcomes is also influenced by social or cultural factors. Achieving a college education may mean more in one culture than another. The factor of satiation should be considered in giving rewards.

Rewards for performance may also change their importance depending upon their exchange value. As tax rates have made current income less valuable, for example, executives have chosen to take deferred or nontaxable rewards. Finally, the extent to which outcomes are valued depends to some degree upon whether they are judged to be fair. Each person tends to compare what she gives to the job (performance, experience, education, status, etc.) and gets from the job (pay, security, recognition, etc.) with the similar inputs and outcomes of someone else doing a similar kind of job. On this basis, we determine whether our situation is fair or unfair. Beyond some level, either overreward or underreward can reduce the satisfaction with outcomes by making us angry or guilty about them.

Based on this discussion, if you want to increase the motivation of your employees, you should:

- Employ people who value the outcomes which the organization can provide.

- Determine what people *want* and provide that as a reward.

- Match people and jobs so that people like what they are doing (such people reward themselves).

- Provide rewards for performance which continue to be desired.

- Make sure that rewards are seen as fair.

The steps outlined have been demonstrated to be a close approximation to the process that you or I go through in deciding whether or not to exert the effort to perform. The experience which actually follows will exert further influence on the future estimate about being able to perform, the clarity of expected performance, the estimate about performance leading to outcomes, and the value of those outcomes.

Those readers familiar with management by objectives (MBO) systems will recognize the parallel features of these steps with MBO systems. Henry Tosi and Stephen Carroll[6] have done perhaps the best assessment of why MBO programs succeed or fail. They have found, as we might expect from this discussion, that where goals are set clearly and jointly between boss and subordinate and where employees gain desired rewards from achieving the goals, MBO programs enhance performance and job satisfaction. On the other hand, where goals are not clear, are imposed by the boss, or lead to outcomes viewed as unrewarding, the systems are not successful.

The next chapter will show how superiors and subordinates work together to agree on the job to be done and when such participation should or should not be used.

Chapter 8 Decision Making and Problem Solving

A resolution to avoid an evil is seldom framed till the evil is so far advanced as to make avoidance impossible.

Thomas Hardy, *Far From the Madding Crowd*

[An] inner peace of mind occurs at three levels of understanding. Physical quietness seems the easiest to achieve, although there are levels and levels of this too, as attested by the ability of Hindu mystics to live buried alive for many days. Mental quietness, in which one has no wandering thoughts at all, seems more difficult, but can be achieved. But value quietness, in which one has no wandering desires at all but simply performs the acts of his life without desire, that seems the hardest.

    I've sometimes thought this inner peace of mind, this quietness, is similar to if not identical with the sort of calm you sometimes get when going fishing, which accounts for much of the popularity of this sport. Just to sit with the line in the water, not moving, not really thinking about anything, not really caring about anything either, seems to draw out the inner tensions and frustrations that have prevented you from solving problems you couldn't solve before and introduced ugliness and clumsiness into your actions and thoughts. (pp. 288-289)

Robert M. Pirsig, *Zen and the Art of Motorcycle Maintenance.* New York: Bantam Books, 1974.

Individual versus Group Decisions

The folklore of management has a lot to say about whether decisions are better made by individuals or groups. People say, "You can't run an organization by committee"; "If you want something done right, you have to do it yourself"; "Two heads are better than one"; and "Groups make better decisions than individuals." As I said earlier, general rules rarely apply all the time. Sometimes group decisions are better than individual decisions, sometimes not; the question again is "What works when?"

The answer depends upon the specifics involved: "What process is used by a group or individual to make the decision?" "What kind of task are we talking about?" "What are the characteristics of the people who might be involved?" "What are the conditions surrounding the people?" "Does the 'goodness' of the decision depend upon the willingness of people to implement it?"

Tasks in which groups have a good chance of performing better than individuals are those which permit a division of labor among group members, permit productive activity among the participants, and benefit from a variety of contributions from the members. A group can't very well type a letter since they can't divide the labor—only one member can be productive at a time, and a variety of skills is not required. On the other hand, a group might very well do better than an individual if the task is to figure out a solution to lagging performance in an office.

Consider the differences between the following tasks: (1) lifting a heavy object, (2) assembling a product, (3) deciding guilt or innocence in court, (4) estimating the temperature outside a room, (5) selling a product, (6) recalling the name of the twenty-first president, (7) reconstructing a story from memory, and (8) solving an equation. Each of these examples has a different set of characteristics which will affect the relative goodness of individual or group performance.

Let's take some task situations and suggest when the group or the single individual is likely to be superior.

Where the task involves random error around a correct answer, combining several estimates is likely to make the group judgment close to the best solution. For example, if we want to estimate the temperature in the room, the more estimates we collect from informed people, the more likely the average will be close to the correct temperature. The odds of any individual making the correct answer are less than the odds that the group collectively can provide the correct answer. In such cases the best individual judgment cannot exceed the correct answer.

Where the task is the generation of alternatives to a problem, obviously the more people, the more alternatives there will be. In such cases the leader's job is to involve as many people as possible in the process and to facilitate the collection of alternative solutions.

Where the task involves recall of the past, the group will provide a better solution than an individual. By increasing the size of a group in which different people have different contributions to make, the likelihood of a group superiority to individual recall is increased.

Where there is clearly one right answer which can be verified, the group is likely to be superior to an individual. For one thing, the more people involved, the greater are the chances that one member will have the correct answer. In addition, several people can provide information and contribute to the logical process involved.

Where a division of labor is possible and the task requires an integration of effort or skill which one person does not possess, then the group will outperform the individual.

Where the task is one in which work cannot be divided and the individual is capable of performing, the individual will outperform the group. Solving an equation, threading a needle, and typing a letter are such examples.

Where the task involves judgment about issues which are not immediately verifiable, it is possible for the group judgment to exceed the best individual judgment. Judgmental decisions involve a combination of fact and logic which pools the various resources that different people add to a group decision.

All this is common sense, so far. Not so obvious, however, are the process requirements in such settings. Where the tasks involve generating alternatives, or looking for the one right answer, or making estimates, the group should be as large as possible and the difficulty is one of collecting the information. In such cases, I visualize filling a football stadium with people and saying over the loudspeaker, "Hey, up there, we need ideas on how to clean up the air pollution in this city. You have pencils and paper provided; now sit in silence for ten minutes and write down all the ideas you can think of." Called "nominal grouping," this technique of having people write solutions silently in groups was developed by Andre Delbecq and associates.[1] It provides lots of ideas in a short time. It is useful because everyone can be active at the same time on a task which benefits from a variety of information or solutions.

On the other hand, where the task involves balanced discussion among group members and agreement among them, the group should be relatively small and the process should facilitate interaction. For such purposes, a group of five or seven people is recommended. Groups smaller than that have limited resources and less ability to divide labor. In fact, except for sex, a group of two is in many ways the worst size. It is fragile since either party can withdraw and end the group life, and perhaps for that reason the two tend to be overly polite. On the other hand, when groups get much larger than seven, they become more formal, more fragmented into subgroups, and more willing to sacrifice individual member needs.

The process requirements just described suggest that where the task is one which involves getting ideas from people, it is necessary to use a method in which large numbers of people can generate and communicate their ideas. Where the task is one which requires interaction and agreement among people, it is necessary to use a method which involves a relatively small number of people and which facilitates their interaction and agreement. The former case requires that people write or code information individually; the latter case requires that people talk with the other members of a group.

The characteristics of the participants may play a part in

determining the relative success of group performance. This is probably not so important in cases of idea-getting; it is vital in the case of group discussion and judgment. Some people give in to the influence of others and therefore reduce the advantage of group judgment. Such compliant members, compared with the noncompliant ones, typically have less understanding of themselves, lower self-esteem, less understanding of others, and less autonomy. They will respond more to group pressure.

Another characteristic of participants which may help or hinder the outcome of their efforts is their orientation to conflict or problem solving. Some individuals exercise power in group situations, producing conflicts and stalemates; others utilize facts and logic in trying to find a solution, and their efforts may be more easily joined with the efforts of others in a group. I'll say more about this shortly.

Finally, the relative value of a group effort is affected by the extent to which problem characteristics involve considerations of objective quality and considerations of a group's willingness to implement the decisions agreed upon. Norman Maier[2] has suggested that a good decision equals the objective quality of the decision times the acceptance of the decision by those who must implement it. A good decision which no one implements is unsatisfactory. Similarly, a low-quality decision which everyone supports is poor.

The evidence related to this issue indicates that group acceptance will generally be greater if group members participate in decisions which affect them. This means that if I am told what the decision or action is to be, unless I am compliant for some reason, I am less likely to accept and support the decision than in cases where I participate in arriving at the decision. Further, if some *decision mechanism,* like voting, is used to arrive at the decision, I am not likely to be as committed to the outcome as I am when we discuss the decision until a consensus is reached. Voting short-circuits discussion and creativity and may make me angry and unsupportive if I lose the vote.

These quality or acceptance considerations are useful to you as a practicing manager in deciding how to structure a decision. In cases where *quality, but not acceptance, is important*—one alternative may yield more production or more sales or higher pay-off than another—and where you as manager easily can determine the pay-offs of alternatives, you can make the decision yourself. If quality, but not acceptance, is important but you cannot calculate the right answer, some kind of group effort may be useful.

If *both quality and acceptance are important* to the outcome, you should take pains to involve people who can deal with both the facts or goals involved and people whose agreement affects the implementation of the decision. For example, suppose the problem involves which of several kinds of work flow is to be utilized in a group. Some work arrangements will produce more production than others. In addition, no matter which kind of work flow is used, it will be only as good as the willingness of the people to make it work. In such cases you will want to make sure that an alternative which provides good production is selected and that it is acceptable to the people who will use it. It may be wise to agree on something which is less than perfect if it is the only alternative acceptable to the employees.

Where the problem is one involving *only acceptance considerations* and all alternatives are OK to you, then you will want the group to arrive at a decision which is judged to be fair and equitable. For example, if the problem is which of three persons in a typing pool is to get a new typewriter, you'll want the typists, with or without your involvement, to arrive at an acceptable decision. If the issue is *low in quality and acceptance considerations,* it is best to use a simple decision mechanism such as flipping a coin to settle the issue.

If all of these considerations seem like a nest of snakes to you, just be patient. In the next chapter I'll indicate one way to put most of them together to show what works when. I'll give you a model which shows what kind of decision process a leader should use under different circumstances.

Problem Solving and Conflict
As has been implied in the previous discussion, problem solving essentially involves "how to" questions. "How can we

increase profits?" "How can we provide better service to our clients?" "How can you find a better job, or a happier life, or a sense of achievement?" Decision making, in contrast, involves a choice. "Which alternative will give us more profit?" "Which method will generate better customer service?" "Which approach will give you more satisfaction?" Both decision making and problem solving are concerned with the exercise of fact and logic.

Conflict, on the other hand, is an exercise of power whether in the form of competitive games or in the form of a fight. The difference between these exercises of power is that games are controlled by a set of rules and have a clear point of termination; fights, on the other hand, have no rules and it is difficult to tell when they have ended. Given our distinction between problem solving and conflict, it is useful to consider three basic ideas which govern their use.

Knowledge is unlimited, but our perception of knowledge is very limited. It helps me to realize that there is a way to do or accomplish anything, anything at all. The limit to solving problems is simply the limit of people's perception and the costs that they are willing to pay or can pay to find an answer. The limits of our perception are illustrated in the conditions of conflict. Most disagreements are *arguments about two solutions,* with no discussion of problems or objectives. You say to your spouse, "Do you want to go to a movie tonight?" Spouse says, "No." You say, "You never want to do what I want to do!" Spouse says, "The only person you care about is yourself." The two solutions are going and not going to a movie.

Another way that our perceptions affect conflict or problem-solving behavior is our tendency to see things as a fixed pie, where one person's gain is at another person's expense. The two solutions of "going to a movie or not" represent a fixed pie. One person gains, and the other loses. In contrast, if the question were stated, "How can we meet your needs *and* my needs?" the situation would be open to problem solving and the pie would no longer be fixed. There are some kinds of problems which must be treated as fixed pies simply because our perceptions can conceive of nothing else.

Experience will demonstrate, however, that in many cases further examination will show approaches which permit the problem solution to benefit both parties involved.

It is becoming more common for labor and management to distinguish between issues which seem to require a gain on one side at the cost of another and those which permit both sides to gain. The former involves what is called distributive bargaining (really, conflict), because what is perceived as a fixed pie—say, a sum of money—must be divided between labor and management in some way. The assumption is that the more money paid out in wages, the less profit there will be to management. Issues in bargaining which are not seen as a fixed pie involve what is called integrative bargaining (really, problem solving), because the solution to the problem may benefit both parties. Finding a way to move a plant so that both the employees and the company benefit is an example of integrative bargaining.

Past behavior is self-rewarding. The second idea means that just repeating past behavior has certain built-in rewards. Or, conversely, trying new behavior has some costs attached. Old behavior is comfortable, predictable, tried and true. New behavior may be uncomfortable, has unpredictable consequences, and is awkward. Perhaps for this reason people use methods for resolving differences that are not particularly good, just because they have been taught those methods and have lots of practice with them. Such methods involve dominance and submission as well as compromise.

The process that we have learned might well be called The Ethic of the Good Loser. The logic goes something like this:

> In a disagreement, there has to be a winner and a loser;
> The loser isn't going to be me;
> So, you will have to lose;
> But losers can make trouble;
> So, I'll tell you that you are bad (evil) if you complain about your loss.

Guilt is a powerful force, as our churches, schools, businesses, and other institutions have demonstrated. One way to illustrate its force is to ask a person to list five rules which her parents taught her in childhood. These say, "You are bad or evil if you . . . ." We get our own set of rules at an age when we can't check them out and may spend lots of years in later life trying to overcome their consequences.

I said that we learn dominance and submission plus compromise through the Ethic of the Good Loser. Here is how it works. We are born into the world innocent and free of guilt. Soon we are told, "Honor thy father and thy mother," "Do what you are told," or "Your father is the boss around here." Which is to say, you are bad if you don't follow orders (be a Good Loser). The whole business may be justified by saying, "Someday you will be a parent yourself, and you will understand." Thus the system will be perpetuated.

Alternatives to the Good Loser Ethic in the family include family meetings in which each person agrees on rules that apply to family members, discussions to solve problems which are not based on the parent as a boss, and an exercise of arbitrary authority by a parent *only* where there is a clear, demonstrable danger to a child.

Then, we enter the school system, and we are told, "Don't ask why, just obey the teacher," and "Learn what you are told to learn," and "The teacher knows best." This Good Loser system is explained by the teacher, "Some of you will be teachers someday, and then you will understand why this is necessary." Which is to say, be a Good Loser now, and when you become a teacher, you can be a Winner and have your own set of Good Losers and perpetuate the system.

Alternatives to this ethic in the classroom are common these days. They include learning communities in which everyone—students and teachers—decide on learning objectives; systems which permit the student to develop an individual program and to progress at his own speed; and systems in which students evaluate their education and partially control the rewards that are given to the teachers.

Finally, we enter employment and are told, "Don't challenge authority," and "Keep your nose clean," and "Do what you are told." The explanation is, of course, that if you do what you are told, you'll get promoted and have your own set of Good Losers.

Alternatives to this system are processes in which people in supervisory positions work out joint agreements with subordinates about expected performance, systems in which everyone in the organization meets to agree on the rules for the economic community, or organizations in which necessary leadership positions are filled by rotation or election from organization members.

All this may sound like moralizing; it isn't meant to do so. The argument is better made on selfish or economic grounds than it is on morals. There are enough facts on the issue for me to argue that if someone can change a person's self-esteem from feeling like a Winner to feeling like a Loser, that person can reduce the other's energy, creativity, and measured intelligence! If you are an employer, it is in your interest to have employees who are as energetic, creative, and intelligent as possible.

The way out of the Good Loser Ethic is to demonstrate and practice ways for people to relate to each other which are based on cooperation and mutual respect. Issues which develop can be resolved with problem solving, not with dominance and submission. Then we will be accustomed to behaving in more productive ways than we are now.

When issues arise, we have a choice of resolving them through conflict or through problem-solving methods. I emphasize, in situations which can lead to disagreement you as manager have a clear choice—will you use conflict methods or problem-solving methods? Looking at Figure 2 (page 92) will help you differentiate the two processes.

I am indebted to Ken Thomas[3] at Stanford University for this nice diagram. Line X, which runs from the upper left-hand corner to the lower right-hand corner, represents a fixed-pie situation in which whatever I gain you lose. Point A on the line means that I get everything and you get nothing; Point B is the reverse. Suppose that we fight about who is to get an orange that both of us want. If I win, I get the whole

Figure 2. Conflict Methods and Problem-Solving Methods†

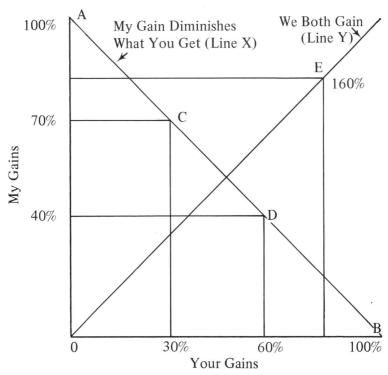

†Adapted from "Conflict and Conflict Management" by K. Thomas, in M. D. Dunnette, ed. *Handbook of Industrial and Organizational Psychology*. Chicago: Rand McNally, 1976.

thing (Point A); if you win, you get the whole thing (Point B).

We may also believe that sharing is good, or half a loaf is better than none. In this case, we will be somewhere on the line between A and B. At Point C, for example, I get part of the orange and you get part. Perhaps we decide to divide the orange. If we argue or bargain about the shares, then you will be trying to move me from Point C to Point D, increasing your share and decreasing mine. Whatever we do, as long as we are moving somewhere on Line X, one person's loss is at the other's gain and the sum of both persons' outcomes is always 100 percent. The whole process of moving each other back and forth on Line X is one of *power*. No facts, no logic, no problem solving—just an exercise of power.

Line Y in the diagram is a whole different trip. On that line we both increase our gains as we move from the lower left-hand corner to the upper right-hand corner. Once it crosses Line X, Line Y represents points in which the total gain to you *and* me is greater than it is at any point on Line X. The ability to move on Line Y depends upon problem solving and the use of *facts* and *logic*.

In the case of the orange, we may wish to engage in problem solving instead of conflict, so we would be moving on Line Y instead of Line X. As a start, we need to know the purpose or objective of the alternatives we have been arguing about. I say to you, "Why do you want the orange?" You say, "I am going to bake a cake and need the orange peel for it. Why do you want the orange?" I say, "I want to make orange juice." In this case the solution is obvious; I take the pulp, and you take the peel.

There may be cases in which you don't want to problem solve. In fact, conflict is fine in some instances. Conflict has the advantage of being exhilarating and emotional; problem solving does not. Conflict is also a way to test one's skills. It is not particularly helpful, however, where one needs the cooperation of the defeated party to carry out a desired action and it does not foster understanding of the outcome by the parties. In contrast, problem solving is useful where one wants creative solutions, commitment to the agreement by those involved, and maximum understanding of the problem. In general, problem solving is preferred where the parties involved need each other's cooperation.

Don't confuse problem solving and conflict. Occasionally I have had people say, "Filley, I tried problem solving with an associate and it didn't work." I say, "Tell me about what happened." The person says, "Well, I sat down with the (expletive) and said . . . ." I say, "*Wait a minute.* It doesn't sound to me like you want a mutually acceptable solution; you sound hostile." The person says, "Yes, I guess I really wanted to shoot him down."

Conflict and problem solving are simply two alternate ways for dealing with situations. The conflict methods are well practiced; the problem-solving methods often are not. The main ingredients for problem solving seem to be:[4]

An expenditure of time. Problem solving often takes more time than domination (forcing) or compromise (splitting the difference).

A set of skills. Problem solving requires knowledge of procedures which lead to mutually acceptable and high-quality outcomes.

Equal power or the absence of power. Where power is balanced or the parties choose to ignore power differences, then both can be involved equally.

A set of beliefs. The parties must believe in the value of cooperation and feel that it is beneficial for both to get what they want.

Awareness of the cost of not agreeing. People need to be aware of the costs of defeating or suppressing each other. This is clear where they depend on each other to accomplish their needs.

Access to a third party. I'm not sure why, but evidence indicates that a third party can often facilitate problem solving. Perhaps it is the difference in interaction which occurs in two-person as opposed to three-person groups. Perhaps it is the help provided by a neutral third party who can aid in suggesting alternatives or support the use of problem-solving skills. I don't know. I only know that marriage counselors, consultants, mediators, and others do have an effect on the tendency to problem solve rather than to fight.

Trust. In terms of behavior, people who trust each other give each other information that makes each vulnerable to the other, and they are willing to be influenced by each other. If I don't trust you, I try to control you as much as possible and I don't tell you things that will make me vulnerable to you. Perhaps equally important, if I withhold information from you, whatever my motives, I risk making you *think* that I don't trust you. Employers who say, "We won't give financial information to our employees; they wouldn't understand it" are signaling to their people that they are not to be trusted.

The reality of the choice between problem solving and conflict was brought home to me recently when I observed a production manager and sales manager talking in a meeting room. In past years the two had fought with each other, distorted information given to each other, and blamed each other for their own problems. As a result of training in problem-solving methods, to be mentioned later in this chapter, my associates and I had introduced the *ability* to problem solve if the people in the company wished to do so.

In this case the discussion went like this:

Production Manager: "Bob, I asked you to meet with me because I need your help. I've listed five orders on the blackboard that we aren't going to be able to get out on time."
Sales Manager: "Let me look them over . . . . Well, Jim, I'll level with you. Three of those orders are never going to be repeat business. We just fell into them. If the customers get angry, I'll take the heat. Two of the orders, though, are from good customers. We just have to get them out on time."
Production Manager: "That's a big help. Let's talk about how we can get them out."
Sales Manager: "Would extra manpower help?"
Production Manager: "It sure would."
Sales Manager: "How about getting some of those new guys in Engineering to help out temporarily?"
Production Manager: "Let's see, we could work overtime, too. But, first, let's go talk to the people in Engineering to see if they will agree to do some temporary work for us."
Sales Manager: "OK, do you have time now?"

This may not seem like much to you. But to me, having seen organizations waste resources through fighting between key people, the change just illustrated was exciting and pleasing. Real changes in behavior are still an awesome thing to see.

Some Essentials for Problem Solving
The steps in problem solving are not complicated, or new for that matter. They just require understanding and practice. As they apply here, I am assuming that two people or groups of people have been on the road to conflict and wish to change to a problem-solving process. Drawing from my own earlier book,[5] I'd suggest the following:

1. *Review and alter the conditions, the perceptions, and the feelings of the people involved.* People engaged in conflict tend to describe a we-they distinction between each other (e.g., labor versus management, sales versus production, day shift versus night shift). Each party also distorts the picture of themselves and the others (We are the good guys; they are the bad guys). Finally, each party may have feelings of threat, defensiveness, or anger which will interfere with problem solving.

Where any or all of these characteristics exist, they must be dealt with before any discussion of goals and solutions begins. We-they distinctions can be reduced if the parties are brought together to identify their needs, with particular emphasis on shared needs. To the extent that the parties can focus upon written statements on a single piece of paper or blackboard, they are beginning to think, "How can we defeat the problem?" instead of "How can we defeat you?" It is important not to discuss solutions at this point since the purpose is to stress commonality of interests. Face-to-face discussions about how each party perceives the other can do much to reduce distortions and hostile or fearful feelings.

The language of problem solving is descriptive and not judgmental. The parties must be able to describe their own feelings and to give descriptive feedback to others in a way that is not offensive. For example, to say, "I disagree with you" is descriptive and usually elicits the response, "Why?" In contrast, to say, "You are wrong" is a judgment and may elicit the response, "No, you are wrong!" Judgments like right, wrong, unfair, stupid, autocratic, or poor-communicator have little value in problem solving. If someone says to you, "You are an autocrat," the situation may be made descriptive by saying, "What behavior of mine do you judge to be autocratic?" Where the problems of judgmental language are serious, I'd recommend a careful study of a book on what is called Transactional Analysis. Two suitable and easily read sources are *I'm OK, You're OK: A Practical Guide to Transactional Analysis,* by Thomas Harris,[6] and *Born to Win,* by M. James and D. Jongeward.[7]

2. *Identify the goals, needs, and values of each party.* Once the parties are ready to focus on a problem instead of each other and have the ability to use descriptive language, the next step is to identify the problem. Perhaps most important here is the question, "To do or accomplish what?" I have already pointed out that people will focus on solutions. The first step is usually one of moving back from solutions to problems. For example, when a manager says to his boss, "I need another secretary," the boss may acquiesce (no conflict), argue (conflict), or ask the manager for the purpose. If the boss says, "To do or accomplish what?" the answer could be "To handle the overload that happens each week in my department." Then the need may be met with one of several solutions.

The needs of both parties should be included equally in a problem-solving discussion. Suppose that I arrive at a hotel with a guaranteed reservation in my hand and the desk clerk says, "I'm terribly sorry, sir, but some of our guests didn't check out as expected and we have no room for you." One method I can use is to fight for my solution: "Look, you rat, get me into this hotel or else!" This has a predictable response: "We have no room." Another method is to say, "Our problem, then, is where am I going to sleep tonight." The odds favor a better outcome for both the clerk and me with the latter method.

The word "values" was purposely included in element Number 2. If I tell my daughter to eat her spinach at the dinner table, it does not change anything for me to say, "You'll like it." A better approach may be to accept the tastes and values of others and to define the problem in a way that respects individual differences. Perhaps in this instance the real problem could be stated, "What foods can we serve that are both nourishing (my need) and taste good (your need)?"

3. *Make an exhaustive search for solutions.* People have a tendency to stop with the first solution which seems acceptable. There are two problems with that behavior. First, the search process should take place without any evaluation of the alternatives generated. Second, experience will show that continued search will often generate a far better solution than the one which would have been accepted. This is the point at which you need to get all solutions possible. As explained earlier in this chapter, tap the brains of a lot of people. The more people, the greater the likelihood that you will find the ideal solution (knowledge is unlimited).

4. *Agree on the solution by consensus.* Where large numbers of people are involved, it may be necessary to choose a solution by voting. The danger with voting, however, is that it ends with a winning group and a losing group, and this win-lose outcome contains the we-they element and may undermine the acceptance of the solution. As already noted, groups which vote tend to short-circuit careful discussion of the alternatives with a process like sticking their hands in the air. Where possible, I'd recommend discussion of the alternatives until one is reached which has sufficient quality and is not unacceptable to anyone.

The consensus rules which aid in this respect are: (a) don't vote, trade, average, flip a coin, etc.; keep talking until a suitable solution is reached; (b) don't argue for your own position; generate facts and logic; (c) don't give in only to reach agreement, but stand up for your own needs until a solution is found which is acceptable to you; and (d) use descriptive language rather than judgmental language in discussing the issues; ask people for information, and provide further information yourself.

The alternative methods of one-man rule or voting are faster, but experience will demonstrate that for some kinds of situations consensus decisions will have high quality, high acceptance, and will generate more creativity, understanding, and commitment.

Since there are obviously lots of cases where one-man rule or some other decision-making method seems to be effective, you may be wondering at this point what works when. The next chapter will put the pieces together to answer that question.

Summary

For the present we can summarize by saying that if you as manager wish to improve your decision-making and problem-solving skills, you should:

- Get information from a large group of people when the issue is one of canceling out random error, generating alternatives, recalling information, or searching for a verifiable solution.

- Use a small group of five or seven people where balanced discussion and judgment are required.

- Make the decision yourself where you can determine the quality and when acceptance by others is not important to its implementation.

- Use a decision mechanism which is appropriate to the relative importance of quality and acceptance considerations.

- Avoid limiting perception to two solutions and a fixed pie. (Ask, *"How* can we do it?" not "Can we do it?")

- Develop problem-solving skills.

- Choose to problem solve when the situation warrants.

- Avoid we-they distinctions.

- Deal with perceptions and feelings before attempting to solve the problem.

- Learn to use descriptive rather than judgmental language.

- Turn choices between two solutions into joint statements of needs, goals, and values.

- Attempt to meet the needs of both parties in a potential conflict situation.
- Make an exhaustive search for solutions.
- Avoid premature judgment of solutions.
- Seek a consensus solution.

Chapter 9 A Road Map for Decision Making

The difficulty in life is choice.

George Moore, *The Bending of the Bough,* Act IV

The Author's Experience
I chose an academic career because it looked like fun and it seemed to me that I could succeed in it. I figured that if I applied the same effort to the academic world that I had directed to selling—assuming I had the necessary ability—I'd just have to succeed. Like most general rules, the idea of success from hard work was partly right, partly wrong. Some people work hard running in circles. Others seem to think that brute force is a substitute for skill. I've learned that basically I am a plodder; in the parable of the tortoise and the hare, I'm the tortoise. I've learned that because I am a plodder, I have to keep at it, I have to know where I want to go, and I have to conserve energy and work efficiently toward my goals.

I conserve a lot of energy by working on things that I understand and that I enjoy. People seem to think that "publish or perish" means that academicians are somehow forced to do research or writing, that it is some kind of threat. The rule really means that effective job performance, including publication, will be rewarded. The people I know in the academic world who *do* feel that they must produce often find research or writing to be so unpleasant that they produce little and are unrewarded. Such people ought to do something else—but that's their problem.

Perhaps the most stressful and energy-wasting behavior on my part is an occasional desire to change someone else. It is an awful feeling to see someone engage in behavior that is ineffective or self-destructive when I know a better way. For me, it has sometimes been like seeing someone who is about to be run over by a truck, grabbing the person to pull him out of the way, discovering that the person *wants* to do it that way, and getting run over *myself.*

These days I try to make the information available if people want it and to respond when people *ask* for help. My biggest problem now is that I don't know what to do about the inability of some people to discriminate between situations or information. Relying on information that just isn't correct is another way to get run over by a truck. To rely on Maslow's "hierarchy of needs,"[1] or on *The Peter Principle,* [2] when neither has a basis in fact, can be terribly misleading. Little wonder that managers suspect academic output and that they talk about the difference between theory and practice or the academic way versus the real world.

My contact with professional managers occurs through research, training, and consulting. I've learned much from the practitioners I meet, and I've met a lot of interesting ones: a man who made red contact lenses for chickens; the inventor of the aerosol can; a religious man who makes roach clips and hash pipes; a major wine producer; and a Texas promoter who owns a hospital, a gravestone company, a funeral parlor, and a graveyard.

A few years ago in a training program I met a real, old-fashioned peddler. He reminded me of the peddlers of patent medicines, turning old ingredients into new products. This man had worked for a luggage manufacturer. To demonstrate the strength of his luggage, he arranged a big promotion with an auto dealer and a department store.

At midnight he was in the front window of a major department store with the store's owner, jacking up a new car to be placed on four pieces of luggage, one under each tire. The radio and newspaper promotion was scheduled to run the next day. A small crisis developed when it was found that the car crushed the luggage. The store owner said, "What are we going to do?" The peddler said, "We are going to get some bricks to fill the suitcases, that's what." Apparently the promotion was a huge success, and it was imitated in other parts of the country. Naturally, panicked salesmen from the company called the peddler to ask how he managed to put a car on four suitcases. He simply told them, "You have to be very careful."

This same man showed up in my training program with a small plastic bucket. He had purchased several thousand of them from a manufacturer. They had not worked out for their original purpose, and they seemed to have no other use. They were too large to be used as litter buckets for autos and too small to be wastebaskets. He wanted to give them value again and asked everyone in the group for possible new uses. I was impressed by the fact that he clearly differentiated his style of decision making. He knew when to make a decision himself, he knew when to get ideas from others, and he later demonstrated his ability to reach consensus in small discussion groups.

What Works When:
Applying the Vroom-Yetton Model*

As suggested in the last chapter, the proper use of different types of decision making can improve the quality of decisions, can increase the likelihood of their understanding and support, and can save time. Fortunately, a road map for proper use of decision-making approaches has been developed by Victor Vroom and Philip Yetton[3] at Yale University. This set of guidelines serves to put together the information developed in the last chapter in a way that helps a manager to know what works when.

Table 1. Types of Management Decision Styles†

AI   You solve the problem or make the decision yourself, using information available to you at that time.

AII   You obtain the necessary information from your subordinates, then decide on the solution to the problem yourself. You may or may not tell your subordinates what the problem is in getting the information from them. The role played by your subordinates in making the decision is clearly one of providing the necessary information to you, rather than generating or evaluating alternative solutions.

CI   You share the problem with relevant subordinates individually, getting their ideas and suggestions without bringing them together

---

*What follows is a summary of the work by Vroom and Yetton. Where I have made substantive changes to their contribution, I also have included Vroom and Yetton's original statements.

†From *Leadership and Decision Making* by V. H. Vroom and P. W. Yetton. Pittsburgh, PA: University of Pittsburgh Press, 1973. Used with permission.

as a group. Then *you* make the decision that may or may not reflect your subordinates' influence.

CII You share the problem with your subordinates as a group, collectively obtaining their ideas and suggestions. Then *you* make the decision that may or may not reflect your subordinates' influence.

GII You share a problem with your subordinates as a group. Together you generate and evaluate alternatives and attempt to reach agreement (consensus) on a solution. Your role is much like that of chairman. You do not try to influence the group to adopt "your" solution and you are willing to accept and implement any solution that has the support of the entire group.

Notice the five decision styles listed in Table 1 (from Vroom and Yetton). Of the five, two types (AI and AII) involve your making the decision and announcing it, even though in AII you may seek information from subordinates; two types (CI and CII) require that you consult with subordinates for ideas and suggestions before making a decision; and one method (GII) requires problem solving with subordinates as described in Chapter 8. The choice of one of these five methods depends upon several considerations:

Whether or not quality is important in the decision. The quality factor means that on purely objective measures one alternative is likely to be better than another. For example, the question may be: Will Alternative A provide greater profit than Alternative B?

Whether or not you have enough information or expertise to make a high-quality decision yourself. Basically, this means whether or not you have the facts and ability to calculate the quality of each possible alternative.

Whether or not the problem is structured. In structured problems the decision maker knows what information is needed and where to get it. In such cases, one merely follows prescribed procedures. Unstructured problems do not have clear procedures and require some kind of group effort to solve them.

Whether or not acceptance is important for implementing the decision. If the decision won't be successful unless people make it work and are committed to its implementation, then acceptance is important.

Whether or not an autocratic decision would be accepted by subordinates. The reasons for this could vary. Some subordinates may accept any direction. Others may see that the boss' decision is obviously correct. Some may feel that they don't have the right to participate in decisions. Whatever the reason, the issue in this case is whether subordinates will go along with the boss' decision.

*Whether or not a mutually beneficial solution is likely to be possible.** If a problem-solving approach can be used to provide a gain for the employees and you, the superior, a mutually beneficial solution is possible. If the decision requires that one side gains while the other loses, a conflict is likely and a mutually beneficial solution is not possible.

Whether or not subordinates will be able to agree with each other about the proposed solution. ** Where subordinates choose to engage in problem solving, they should be able to agree with each other. If they choose to engage in conflict, they probably cannot agree.

Based on the preceding factors, the proper approach to use depends upon the following rules:

1. *The Information Rule:* When the quality of the decision is important and you do not have enough information or expertise to solve the problem, don't make the decision yourself. (Don't use AI.)

---

*The Vroom-Yetton model asks, "Do subordinates share the organizational goals to be obtained in solving the problem?" (Vroom and Yetton, 1973, p. 186). This is sensible, but if we consider job performance as the organizational goal and employee satisfaction as the employee goal, the logic is consistent with our earlier discussion on motivation.

**The Vroom-Yetton model asks, "Is conflict among subordinates likely in preferred solutions?" (Vroom and Yetton, 1973, p. 216).

2. *The Boss-Subordinate Conflict versus Problem-Solving Rule:** If the quality of the decision is important and subordinates are likely to engage in conflict with you rather than problem solving, you will need final control over decision quality. (Don't use GII.)

3. *The Unstructured Problem Rule:* Where quality is important, you lack the necessary information to solve the problem, and the problem is unstructured, you will need to use methods which require interaction with subordinates. In such cases some form of group discussion is the most efficient. (Don't use AI, AII, or CI.)

4. *The Acceptance Rule:* If acceptance by subordinates is critical to implementation and they are not likely to accept your autocratic decision, don't impose your own decision on them. (Don't use AI or AII.)

5. *The Subordinate-Subordinate Interaction Rule:*** If acceptance is critical, your autocratic decision is not likely to be accepted, and subordinates must all support the decision if it is to work, then you will need to use methods which permit interaction of subordinates. (Don't use AI, AII, or CI.)

6. *The Fairness Rule:* If quality is important, acceptance is critical, and acceptance won't occur with your autocratic

---

*The Vroom-Yetton model calls this the "Trust Rule," saying, "If quality is important and subordinates can't be trusted to base their efforts to solve the problem on organization goals, GII is eliminated ...." (Vroom and Yetton, 1973, p. 33). In other words, if subordinates engage in a win-lose conflict between their own goals and those of the organization, the benefits of their participation will have to be partially sacrificed by limiting their participation to making suggestions rather than coming to agreement on the decision.

**The Vroom-Yetton model calls this the "Conflict Rule" and suggests that in spite of the need for conflict or problem solving, the subordinates will have to agree on the solution if their acceptance is necessary for its success.

decision, group problem solving is required. (Don't use AI, AII, CI, or CII.)

7. *Acceptance Priority Rule:* If acceptance is important, subordinates are not likely to accept your autocratic decision, and a mutually beneficial outcome is likely, then use group problem solving. (Don't use AI, AII, CI or CII.)

This same information is put together in a road map for decision making in Figure 3 (page 110) (from Vroom and Yetton). By starting at the left side and answering each of the yes-no questions, you will be led to a number. That number tells you a problem type, and the appropriate methods to be used for that type of problem are listed in Table 2. For example, problem Type 1 occurs when there is no quality re-

Table 2. Problem Types and the Feasible Set of Decision Processes†

Problem Type	Acceptable Methods
1.	AI, AII, CI, CII, GII
2.	AI, AII, CI, CII, GII
3.	GII
4.	AI, AII, CI, CII, GII*
5.	AI, AII, CI, CII, GII*
6.	GII
7.	CII
8.	CI, CII
9.	AII, CI, CII, GII*
10.	AII, CI, CII, GII*
11.	CII, GII*
12.	GII
13.	CII
14.	CII, GII*

*Within the feasible set only when the answer to question F is yes.

†From *Leadership and Decision Making* by V. H. Vroom and P. W. Yetton. Pittsburgh, PA: University of Pittsburgh Press, 1973. Used with permission.

Figure 3. Decision-Process Flow Chart†

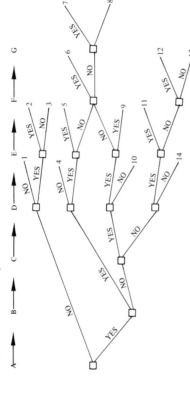

A. Is there a quality requirement such that one solution is likely to be more rational than another?
B. Do I have sufficient information to make a high-quality decision?
C. Is the problem structured?
D. Is acceptance of decision by subordinates critical to effective implementation?
E. If I were to make the decision by myself, is it reasonably certain that it would be accepted by my subordinates?
F. Is a mutually acceptable solution likely?
G. Is conflict among subordinates likely in preferred solutions?

†From *Leadership and Decision Making* by V. H. Vroom and P. W. Yetton. Pittsburgh, PA: University of Pittsburgh Press, 1973. Used with permission.

quirement (Question A) and the acceptance by subordinates is not critical to the implementation (Question D). In such cases any of the five methods of decision making (Table 2) are acceptable. None of the preceding seven rules will be violated with any of the decision-making methods.

At this point you will have to consider some other things. For example, in problem Type 1, the fastest method is likely to be for you to make the decision yourself (AI). This may be fine in the short run, but you pay the cost of failing to develop subordinate participation and problem-solving skills. Vroom has shown that managers underutilize the problem-solving method (GII), and my guess is they bypass it because people don't have enough practice and skill with problem solving (The Ethic of the Good Loser). Even at the cost of time, it may be important to develop problem-solving skills in relatively easy and unstressful situations so they may be used more easily later on more complicated issues.

Now let's take a real case and trace it through the model. In a company making pumps, the driveway surrounding the loading dock area has become cracked and worn. The president, John Calkin, is certain that it needs replacement, but he is confused by the fact that bids from three contractors vary by $1500 and by a possibility that the company will want to change the location of the loading area if a planned addition to the plant is made. The plant addition will take place only if sales increase during the next two years.

Calkin's subordinates are the plant manager, the sales manager, the head of the engineering department, and the controller. Each has some information to contribute to the solution of the problem, but neither the group nor any individual has the answer to the problem.

In talking to Calkin, the questions in the Vroom-Yetton model were asked. Here are his answers:

A. Is there a quality factor? Yes

B. Do you have sufficient information to make a high-quality decision? No

C. Is the problem structured? No

D. Is acceptance of decision by subordinates critical to effective implementation? No

In this case the decision type is 14; the manager should call a meeting to collect ideas or suggestions (CII) or should utilize problem solving with them (GII).

As a final illustration, let us take a case developed by Norman Maier.[4] The situation involves three workers and a foreman named Gus who work on a pump assembly operation. The three workers are paid on group piecework, and each worker has different times on the three stations of the assembly operation. At present the three workers rotate the positions each hour to relieve boredom. A time study of the group indicates that if each group member stayed at his best position, production could be increased substantially.

According to the road map for decisions, the following answers would be given:

A. Is there a quality factor? Yes

B. Does the foreman (manager) have sufficient information to make a high-quality decision? Yes

D. Is acceptance by subordinates critical to implementation? Yes

E. If the foreman (manager) were to make the decision by himself, is it reasonably certain that the decision would be accepted by the subordinates? No

F. Is a mutually acceptable solution possible? Yes

The result is decision Type 6. The foreman should use problem solving for his solution. Some degree of quality may necessarily be sacrificed, say, by having each worker rotate his two best positions, if that method is more acceptable than having each stay in his best position. Maier clearly demonstrates that if the group takes a choice approach, defining the problem as a choice between the old method (rotate every hour) and the new method (each stays in his best position), the result is rarely a creative solution that satisfies both the workers and the foreman. On the other hand, if the foreman takes a problem-solving approach, a creative solution is likely. In the problem-solving approach, the issue might be stated as follows: What work method can we agree to that will increase production, be satisfying, and keep our team together? Stated this way, the problem yields a number of possible solutions.

Besides the advantages of improving the quality and acceptance of decisions, the use of this road map for decision making should help you to use your time most efficiently. Where problem-solving skills are not present in your organization, it is a good idea to develop them. In the next chapter, I want to discuss some methods of time saving which will free more time to be used for productive purposes.

Chapter 10   Managing Your Time — Analysis and Control

"Would you tell me, please, which way I ought to go from here?"
"That depends a good deal on where you want to go," said the Cat.
"I don't much care where," said Alice.
"Then it doesn't matter which way you go," said the Cat.

Lewis Carroll, *Alice in Wonderland*

Styles of Dealing with Time
A few years ago I decided to review the literature on the subject of time management written in the past ten years. I did so because I began to realize that I was a rotten manager of my own time. I have always believed that if one is unhappy about something, he should do something about it. I really have little patience for the whiners and crybabies who wallow in their own despair without doing anything to make things better. Since I was messy with time, I tried to improve my management of it.

As I thought about the subject it seemed to me that I could identify at least five styles of dealing with time. First, there is the person who is bored with life in general. Such people seem to hate to work, but when they have leisure, they find it boring too. I picture them as waiting around for their own death. Second, there are the happy people who enjoy their leisure and put out the necessary work to maintain employment. Like the first type, this kind of person is in a rut, but for her the rut is satisfying. The third type is the nose-to-the-grindstone person. Such people seem to believe that brute force will help them meet their goals, so they spend little time in leisure. They are convinced that hard work will inevitably lead to accomplishment.

I was an example of the third type. I worked long hours. I was irritated at friends and students who interrupted me. Some days I just seemed to spin around, starting one thing, then starting another, and not finishing anything. I was like the person who tries to meet his living expenses by always increasing his income, although it may be easier to reduce expenses. I would go home at night exhausted, with the vague feeling that I really hadn't accomplished very much for all my effort.

The fourth style for dealing with time is the person who is conscious of time, views it as a precious commodity, and feels guilty if it is wasted. Such people seem to be active and productive, both in their work and their leisure. Finally, there are those who consciously plan and manage their time. They map out their goals and time allocations, accomplishing the things that are most important to them. I'd like to suggest how this type operates.

Time Personality

Let's notice that each of us has a time personality. By this I mean that we as individuals have distinctive patterns of time use which we have acquired or which are part of our physiology. These patterns need to be identified if we are to have a basis for change. I like to think of time personality as containing two parts. The first part involves public time—that is, how we deal with the time expressed by the clock on the wall—the external clock. Public time is like the red light meaning stop. We all decide that we'll break the day into twenty-four hours, and we agree that for our part of the country nine o'clock will be the same spot on the clock for everyone.

The second part of time personality involves our internal clock. As individuals, we have our own ways of perceiving time, based on a mechanism inside of us that runs at our own personal speed. Each person's internal time clock runs at a speed that is different from everyone else's. Later in this chapter I'll show how we can get a picture of the internal clock of ourselves and others.

Public Time

But first, let's consider public time. My review of studies describing how managers use time has given me an impression about typical patterns. If various surveys can be generalized, they suggest that executives:

- Have about fourteen minutes of uninterrupted time each day.
- Spend an average of five hours a week in formal meetings.
- Work about sixty-three hours a week, fifty-three of which are in the office.
- Use verbal communication for 80 percent of messages to others.

- Spend most of their time on short-term tasks.
- Take much of their action at the initiation of someone else.

I have no way of knowing whether these figures are really accurate averages, but my experience in working with executives has indicated that these people would rarely disagree that the preceding pattern describes their own actions.

On this basis, let me describe what a day in the life of Mr. Jones might be like. Mr. Jones, the partner of a small manufacturing company, enters his office at 8:00 a.m. on Monday. As soon as he sits down, his partner walks in with a cup of coffee in his hand and says, "Well, Jim, were the fish biting?" A visitor has just controlled his time. After his partner leaves, Mr. Jones starts to think about a new product that he wants to add. The phone rings, his secretary answers, and the caller says, "Is Mr. Jones busy?" The secretary looks at Mr. Jones and says, "No, I'll ring him." Fourteen minutes have passed, and again Jones' time is controlled externally. The caller says, "Jim, are you free tomorrow morning? I'd like to see you about ten o'clock." Jones says, "That will be fine," and at that point he has split his next morning into two shorter periods.

A foreman enters the office as Jones begins to study his balance sheet. He is there because Mr. Jones has told everyone that he has an Open Door Policy. The foreman says, "Mr. Jones, there is something that I'd like to talk to you about." Jones looks up from his income statement, thinking, "Oh, hell, another interruption!" and says, "What is it!?" The foreman says, "Oh, I guess you're busy, I'll come back later."

The morning passes with calls and visitors and finally the chairperson of the United Fund Drive walks in. The visitor asks if Jones will serve on the executive council for the new solicitation. Jones says, "Gosh, I just don't have the time." (Meaning, I don't want to.) Finally, at noon Jones leaves the office, telling his secretary that he is going to Ella's Beans-and-Brat House for a noon meeting. At that meeting he dribbles catsup on his pants while he tries to eat and talk with three of his managers about the new budget. To settle his lunch, he has one very dry martini and goes back to the office.

The afternoon, too, is filled with visitors, phone calls, meetings, and emergencies, with short periods of rest in between. In some periods Jones tries to take care of correspondence, setting up the dictating machine, answering one or two letters, and putting things away as each new interruption occurs. Finally, at four o'clock things slow down and Jones begins to prepare his report to the board of directors. Tired and uncreative, he begins the most taxing job of the day.

He leaves the office at six and drives an hour to reach his home, listening to The Four Shouters on the radio, as the new rock sensation is thrust upon him with little deliberate choice on his part. At home, his wife says, "Well, Sweetheart, how was your day?" "Busy," he says. "I've been going all day long." "What did you accomplish?" she asks. "I really don't know," says Jones.

If any of that description sounds familiar, you may find this chapter useful. I picture Jones as traveling three miles in one. That is, on the road from the time he enters the office until he leaves, his journey is controlled by other people, looking something like the route in Figure 4.

No wonder he's tired. He has traveled a long way because of the response he's making to others. He might have more energy and efficiency if his trip looked more like the one shown in Figure 5.

To take the easier trip, Mr. Jones would have to learn to manage his time. As I shall be emphasizing throughout this chapter, a major element in time management is to *define a good job*. Let me do that now. If I am successful in preparing this chapter, I will show you how to do the following:

• Get more accomplished in the formal meetings that you have.

• Accomplish more than you do now in fewer hours than you are presently working.

• Increase your amount of nonverbal communication with others.

Figure 4. A Day Controlled by Others

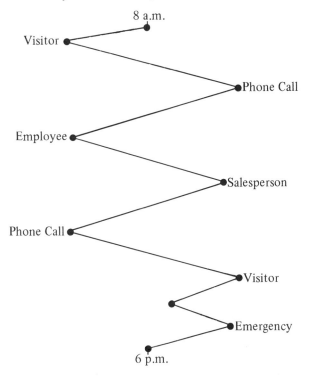

Figure 5. A Day Controlled by Manager

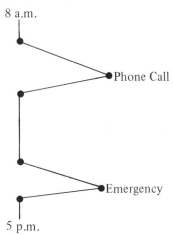

- Reduce the number of short-term tasks which you perform and increase the number of longer-term tasks.

- Increase the degree of control which you have over your own time.

Before we consider the techniques to meet these objectives, we also need to consider our inside clocks. Our internal time system is the other part of our time personality.

The Internal Clock

It appears that our internal clocks are affected by two factors. One is the fairly permanent part of our nature more generally identified as personality. The other has to do with the conditions which may or may not be present in the immediate situation. As a manager, you need to understand the first factor to appreciate how others might react in the same situation. For example, on this basis you can predict which employees are most likely to get bored or fidgety in a long meeting. You also need to know the second factor to adjust conditions to make work seem more pleasant and interesting.

The work on our internal clocks has been nicely summarized by John Orme.[1] He reports studies which investigate relationships between personality or working conditions and measures of time. Two related measures are commonly used. We shall look at one: an estimate of a fixed amount of time. For example, using an external clock (wristwatch), I may ask you to sit silently during a period of time which I will identify by saying "start" at the beginning and "stop" at the end. Then I will ask you to estimate the amount of time which has passed. Evidence suggests that, compared with other people doing the same thing, you will have a tendency to consistently overestimate or underestimate the time passed. In the example given, when I mark off a five-minute interval for you, you may report that two minutes passed. Given a number of trials, we might find that you consistently underestimate the time interval. On the other hand, we would find that other people would consistently say that the time was more than five minutes.

People who underestimate a measured interval of time

are described as having a *slow internal clock*. People who overestimate are described as having a *fast internal clock*. As we shall also see shortly, by changing the situation from one of unfilled time—e.g., sitting in silence—to one of filled time—e.g., listening to music—everyone's estimate of time might be decreased.

Orme has noted some interesting patterns involving the internal clock. Table 3 (page 124) shows some patterns which occur when fast and slow time clock people are compared. As indicated, people with slow time clocks (who say that five minutes have passed when eight minutes have really gone by) are more likely to be introverted. They typically have higher academic achievement than fast time clock people and seem better able to do something now (or refrain from doing something) which will lead to some reward in the future. They engage in more fantasy than fast time clock people and are described by others as slow and careful. Slow time clock people prefer pictures and images which are passive (e.g., clouds in the sky) instead of active (e.g., a dashing waterfall). As expected, they can wait longer in a situation without objection.

In contrast, if you have an employee with a fast time clock, you will expect the person to have more difficulty sitting through a long meeting, more difficulty being inactive, and more difficulty in putting off goals that are desired right now. In managing this person you might be sure to state the ending time of a meeting, keep the person occupied, and break down a long-term goal into steps which can be achieved relatively soon.

Note that one type of time clock is not automatically better than another. Fast and slow time clock people are not differentiated by intelligence or sex. There is some reason to believe that fast time clock people are higher in achievement motivation, though slow clock people also have been shown to have high achievement motivation.

The lower section of Table 3 shows things which may be altered to change the time estimates of everyone, fast or slow clock people. When time is filled, it seems to pass more quickly. That is, if instead of sitting silently, people can ob-

Table 3. Internal Clock Characteristics†

Slow Internal Clock	*Fast Internal Clock*
Underestimates time in fixed interval	Overestimates time in fixed interval
Introverted	Extroverted
Higher academic achievement	Lower academic achievement
Able to exhibit or inhibit behavior for future reward	Can't exhibit or inhibit behavior for future reward
Engages in more fantasy	Engages in less fantasy
Described as slow and careful	Described as quick and careless
Prefers passive images	Prefers active images
Waits longer time without objection	Waits shorter time without objection

Internal clock is slowed (time seems to pass more quickly) with:
1. Filled time rather than unfilled time
2. Difficult rather than easy tasks
3. Interesting rather than boring tasks
4. Stress or pain rather than no stimulation to the senses
5. Passive attitude toward time rather than active attitude toward time.

†Adapted from *Time, Experience and Behavior* by J. E. Orme. New York: American Elsevier, 1969.

serve, hear, or experience something, they will feel that time goes more quickly. As a manager, you might consider avoiding waiting periods and maybe having music or other time-filling ingredients instead. Time passes more quickly with difficult rather than with easy tasks and with interesting rather than uninteresting tasks. As a manager, you might try to challenge people with tasks they like; where the work is routine and boring, you can try to relieve the boredom with job rotation, special assignments, or, perhaps, time off.

Time also passes more quickly under stress or pain and when the person takes a passive attitude toward the passing of time. Creating pain is hardly recommended for management, but employing people less preoccupied with immediacy might be possible. When people are in a rut, changing the job assignment or redesigning the job might also stimulate their interest and performance. If they seem to stay in their rut, the least you can do as a manager is define good levels of performance and reward those that meet or exceed good performance levels.

The Need to Define a Good Job
There is a story in management folklore that involves Charles Schwab, former president of Bethlehem Steel, and Ivy Lee, his consultant. The story illustrates the importance of defining a good job for ourselves as managers. Alec Mackenzie's *The Time Trap* [2] is one source of this often-told story, but the following version is my own reconstruction of what I believe to be a true tale. It seems that Lee was in Schwab's office one day when Schwab said: "Ivy, you tell me how to get more done in a day, and I'll pay you anything within reason." Lee responded, "Charlie, here is a pencil and piece of paper. Write down the ten most important things that you must accomplish tomorrow and rank them in order of their importance. Then, when you come to work tomorrow, start on the first job and stay with it until it is finished. Then, start on the second task and stay with it. Work your way down the list and try to finish it. Even if you can't do everything, you will have accomplished more than you would have without those goals. When you are accustomed to the method, get your people to use it too. Then if you find it worthwhile, send me a check."

According to the story, Schwab sent Lee a check for $25,000. Schwab's friends kidded him about paying so much money for such a simple idea. Schwab responded, "Yes, it is simple, but it may be one of the most important lessons that I have learned." Schwab had learned to define a good job for himself. I expect that when Schwab went home at night, his wife also asked whether he had had a good day. I imagine that Schwab responded, "Yes, I did. I accomplished the ten objectives that I had established as my definition of a good day."

With Schwab's lesson in mind, I'd like to point out the things that you can do to manage your time more effectively. I'd like to start with some steps for establishing a system of time management. Then, I'd like to give you some tips for time saving. You may use any or all of these things to improve your own use of time.

A System for Time Management

Find out your present pattern of time use. The best predictor of future behavior is past behavior in a similar situation. If we are to change behavior, we need to know specifically what our present patterns are now. As a start you need to know specifically what you are doing now. You can get a picture of your internal clock by following one of the procedures mentioned earlier. Repeat this several times and take an average. Chances are you will consistently overestimate or underestimate the actual time interval. Then, see whether the characteristics listed in Table 3 describe your behavior. If they do describe you, then you have a better understanding of your actions and their consequences.

You also will want to determine your pattern of public time use. This can be done in a number of ways. One way is to keep a log. Lawyers and other professionals have sheets that mark off the time of the day. Using such sheets, you can keep a record of what you do and how long each task takes. I'd suggest that you record on such sheets at least every two hours and that you do this for at least a week. Another way is to mark off the week into half-hour intervals and number the intervals from one to eighty. Then, from a table of random numbers or a hat containing eighty numbers on separate pieces of paper, select a sample and have someone come to you at these times and ask what you are doing and how long you have been doing it. These or other methods will give you a picture of your time use.

Once this is done, analyze the results. First, look for tasks that you repeat the same way daily, weekly, or even monthly. Next, look for tasks which could be done just as well by someone else if you were to take the time to train another person. Finally, look for nonproductive periods. Nonproductive time may be spent driving to work, waiting for others, or procrastinating because you don't want to start on something.

Invest time to save time. It is not uncommon to hear a manager say, "Look, it only takes me fifteen minutes a day to rearrange the work orders—I've been doing it for years. It would take me two hours to train someone else to do it." Yet if these two hours were spent, the investment would pay for itself after only eight days, and the manager would have fifteen minutes more each day from then on. Another response I get is the statement that the manager does the task because he has tried to get someone else to do it and that person fouled it up. That kind of situation may be handled by defining a good job for someone else. In many cases, the subordinate didn't mess up the job; the manager gave poor directions. As I have emphasized before, subordinates generally *want* to do a good job for you because you are the person who hands out the rewards. You won't find many people who want to punish or deny themselves.

Given the information from this analysis, you ought to be able to make a list of repetitive tasks and another list of tasks that you can train others to do. That is your agenda. The repetitive tasks can be standardized by developing checklists or by preparing written procedures. Here is an example. In my work with executives I occasionally conduct training programs. Prior to each program, I used to make a list of needed equipment (projectors, screens, flipcharts, pencils, etc.), materials (articles, exercises, questionnaires, etc.), room arrangements, time schedules, additional personnel, and meal or coffee-break arrangements. I've done this for years, and it takes about fifteen to thirty minutes. When I got lazy, I just described these things from memory over the telephone. Either way, something would always be missing or done incorrectly. Then I would complain about how incompetent the local training arrangers were and would wonder if anyone was ever able to do things right. Finally, one day I took four hours and developed a checklist of every conceivable item that would be needed for a training program. Now I just check off the items needed and between my own secretary and the client training arranger, the facilities and materials are complete and in order. It's amazing how much more competent the other people have become!

Besides getting rid of repetitive tasks, you will also want to develop a training schedule for subordinates. By investing your time in training others, you will make their jobs more interesting and will free your own time. I recall a small plastics company with which I once worked. The company made light diffusers for fluorescent fixtures and plastic parts for refrigerators. In one year the company ran two pounds of scrap for every pound of finished product. It seems that when the light diffusers were cut and stored for shipment, many would shrink and become unusable. The problem stemmed from the uncontrolled temperature and humidity in the plant which caused the plastic to shrink when things weren't right.

Although these problems were solvable, the president couldn't get to them because he spent much of his time interviewing applicants for production jobs. He claimed that there wasn't enough time to deal with production problems. By training one of the office people to do the preliminary screening of applicants, the president only had to talk with a fraction of the people who applied for work. The resulting free time was used to solve his other problems.

The time analysis will also highlight periods of nonproductive time. Later in this discussion I'll show how to fill or eliminate those periods through the use of tape recorders or through the elimination of procrastination.

Plan the use of your year, week, and day: define a good job for yourself. Effective time managers define a good year, a good week, and a good day by stating the objectives to be accomplished for each. Annual goals are of two types: those stated as levels of activity and those stated as successful project completion. Activity goals are continuous processes which are expressed as quantity, quality, cost, or comparisons of time. Such standards as return on invested capital, output per manhour, feet per second, scrap rates, or employee turnover are examples. These standards are best broken down into daily, weekly, or monthly figures and monitored for such periods with reports or graphs.

Annual project goals are special activities which have an identifiable completion. In such cases it is important to state the characteristics which will be present or subtasks accomplished if the project is successfully completed. Examples of project goals are completing a feasibility study for a new process, installing a piece of equipment, opening a sales office, and reorganizing the company.

A good week is generally defined as a road map from beginning to end, in which you allocate your activities as units, or blocks of time. In doing this, it is well to keep several ideas in mind. First, there is a time during the day when you are freshest and most creative. If you want to verify this, just ask any ten people to identify the time each day when they are most energized and alert. Most people will respond without hesitation. This optimum period should be used for tasks which require your best intellectual effort. If you are at your best at 8:30 a.m., that time should be used for reading technical reports or creative projects, not 4:00 p.m. when you are dragging. Do your planning and problem solving at the best times and save the routine things, like opening mail or conversations with others, for later.

Another thing to keep in mind while planning your week is that when short-term tasks can be bunched, they can be turned into a single, longer task, and the time formerly used in setting up or breaking down the short-term tasks can be saved. You can do this by trying to make your phone calls in bunches, by seeing visitors in bunches, and by handling correspondence in bunches. Finally, in doing your weekly scheduling, leave some time for reflective thinking. Make appointments with yourself. Then when someone calls and asks if you are busy, your secretary can say, "Yes, he is. Can he call you back between eleven and eleven-thirty?" Experience will show that most people don't object to being put off; they object to ambiguity. If your secretary says, "He'll call you back," the caller is left thinking, "What does that mean—this morning? Next week?"

Table 4 shows two days from a weekly plan for an executive with a peak in the early morning. On Monday she has blocked out the period from 8 to 11 to work on her budget. Her calls will be held until 11. Her lunch is not spent working, and a period from 1 to 4 is provided to meet daily goals that fit. Correspondence is blocked from 4 to 5. She has reserved a period from 1 to 5 on Tuesday to meet with subordinates, abandoning the Open Door Policy in favor of pre-established blocks of time when employees will find her ready and willing to meet with them. More on this later.

Table 4. Sample from a Weekly Plan

Time	Monday	Tuesday
8:00	Work on Budget	Daily Goals
9:00		
10:00		
11:00	Phone Calls	Phone Calls
12:00	Lunch	Lunch
1:00		
2:00	Daily Goals	Meetings with Subordinates
3:00		
4:00	Correspondence	
5:00		

Daily goals represent the third portion of this planning. They are the things which will be fully or partially completed if the day is to be judged successful. Some executives like to use two such lists. The first is "must do." It contains the most important goals. The second is a "can do" list, to be attacked if there is sufficient time. Such lists will allow you to chart your own course through the day and will let you avoid the use of busyness or fatigue as the definition of a good job. Some managers prefer to list their daily objectives the night before; some do it in the morning. I make my own list early in the morning after I exercise and meditate. I run through the whole day in my mind and then make a list of my objectives. Then I try to follow my plan as closely as possible. With some experimenting you will find your own preferred pattern.

Develop nonintrusive methods for dealing with others. Intrusive methods are those in which one party interrupts another; nonintrusive methods are those in which both people are ready to communicate or which permit each party to act when he chooses. For some reason the British are more sensitive to intrusion than Americans, perhaps because they mark off privacy with personal behavior rather than with walls. They are careful about using the telephone—a terribly intrusive instrument—and make much greater use of written messages. When one gets a written message, she can choose her own response to it. For that reason, I recommend the use of handwritten interoffice memos. They don't have to be typed, they give each party a record of the transaction, and they aren't intrusive. Some executives even use handwritten letters on the same type of form.

Other executives make creative use of tape recorders for the same purpose. I know one executive who has provided each of his managers with minicassette recorders. When one person wants to communicate with another, she dictates the message on a cassette, then either sends it through interoffice mail or simply drops it on the other person's desk.

I'd also suggest making your personal meetings nonintrusive. Block out portions of the week to be available to others as shown in Table 4. They can either make an appointment or with a short wait can count on seeing you. In either case both you and the other person are meeting intentionally and willingly. Get your signals straight with others as well. I have met several executives who actually have a signal light on the door which means, "Come in, I'm happy to see you," or "Stay away and don't bother me." It's the old traffic-light principle again.

The next chapter continues with the subject of time management. I'll be talking about how to use meetings more effectively, the process of delegation, and about some other tips for saving time. By the end of that chapter you can determine whether I have done a good job as defined at the beginning of the present one.

Chapter 11   Managing Your Time — Tips for Time-Saving

Tanzan and Ekido were once traveling together down a muddy road. A heavy rain was still falling.

Coming around a bend, they met a lovely girl in a silk komono and sash, unable to cross the intersection.

"Come on, girl," said Tanzan at once. Lifting her in his arms, he carried her over the mud. Ekido did not speak again until that night when they reached a lodging temple. Then he no longer could restrain himself.

"We monks don't go near females," he told Tanzan, *"especially not young and lovely ones. It is dangerous. Why did you do that?"*

"I left the girl there," said Tanzan. *"Are you still carrying her?"*

"Muddy Road," *Zen Bones, Zen Flesh*

In this chapter we will discuss some of the routine elements in a manager's schedule: delegation, meetings, correspondence, and a few miscellaneous items. Having a good system for handling these time-consuming, recurring responsibilities is an important part of effective time management.

Saving Time through Delegation

As an organization grows it becomes increasingly possible to divide the labor, spreading the work over more people. I said it is possible—not that it happens automatically. For efficient work allocation to take place, the organization must be planned, the work or objectives in each job must be identified, and effective delegation must take place. I'll talk about the first two later, but here I want to discuss delegation within the context of time saving. You may have experienced a situation in which the more subordinates you have reporting to you, the more work you have. That doesn't make sense. Presumably, the purpose of adding subordinates is to reduce, not increase, the amount of work you do. The difficulty in accomplishing this is caused, in part, by a lack of understanding and use of delegation skills.

I've already explained the importance of demonstrating to individuals that they can perform the work expected, defining a good job, drawing a clear relationship between performance and rewards, and insuring that rewards chosen are valued by the people doing the work. We haven't talked much about the subtleties of personal interaction, however. My understanding of this process has been aided by the work of William Oncken and D. L. Wass[1] and the basic ideas on delegation which follow are theirs.

Let's look first at the realities of work demands. Part of what we do in our jobs is determined by the boss. She hands out the goodies, has power over rewards and punishments, and assigns work to us that we pretty much have to do. In addition to boss-assigned tasks, we also have responsibilities that are dictated by the work system. For example, the production department responds to requirements created by the sales department, product specifications from engineering, and schedules from production control. The shipping department, in turn, responds to requirements from the production and sales departments.

Finally, we have a range of discretion in our own jobs which includes self-imposed requirements. Some of these self-imposed tasks we pass on to our own subordinates in the form of delegation. They work for us. Presumably, the more subordinates you or I have working for us, the more our capacity for accomplishment of work is increased.

Herein lies the difficulty. Sometimes you begin to work *for* your subordinates. I don't mean work in their interest. I mean do their work for them. Bill Oncken describes the situation in terms of who ends up with the "monkey on his back." The "monkey" is responsibility for performance and, importantly, the *initiative to act.* To illustrate, suppose you ask a subordinate to investigate the costs and benefits of changing the paint used in the production process and to give you a report concerning his recommendations in thirty days. You identify three alternate suppliers to be considered and show the subordinate an example of a similar study done on another material.

Thirty days later the subordinate walks in with catalogues from the alternate suppliers and some cost figures on your present paint use. He says, "I got most of what you wanted, but I haven't had time to put everything together in a report." If you accept the partial report, the subordinate has put the monkey on your back. You will be doing his work for him. The subordinate may even leave saying, "And if you have any questions, let me know." Your efforts to improve operations have left you with more work to do.

Let's take another situation. You pass a subordinate in the hall and he says, "Boss, we have trouble with the dies on the punch press and our scrap rate is way up." You respond, "OK, I'm on my way to a meeting now, but I'll think about this and get back to you." The employee has successfully put the monkey (his problem) on your back and left you with the initiative to act.

As time goes on, you accumulate the monkeys from your subordinates. I can picture you in your office on Saturday morning trying to catch up. You look out the window and there goes a carload of your subordinates on the way to the golf course. They wave and smile. In the car, one person turns to the other and says, "I'd hate to have his job. He never gets caught up."

What can you do? You can take pains to define a good job and to leave subordinates with the initiative. There are various degrees of this, depending upon the situation. Sometimes you will say, "I want you to proceed and to ask me for information if it is needed." Sometimes you will say, "I want you to consider the problem and to recommend a complete plan of action to me for my approval before you enact the plan." Finally, in some cases you will say, "I want you to act on this yourself and to report your results to me." In each of these cases you are leaving the subordinate with the initiative to act.

In the example mentioned earlier, the partially finished report should be returned to the subordinate. To accept it is to reward undesired behavior. To return it is to clarify that such behavior is not appropriate and that a good job is required. The subordinate will learn that turning in partially finished work is costly and requires additional effort on his part.

In the second illustration, you might tell the subordinate to consider the tooling problem and to contact you with a recommendation to solve it. He is left with the initiative to work on the issue and to see you.*

This whole idea of work assignment is known in the military as the doctrine of completed staff work. Basically, it means that when work is assigned to someone, it is that

---

*While writing this chapter I happened to have lunch with a former student of mine who works for the university administration and consults from time to time. As we talked about the subject of time management, we both discussed the Bill Oncken article I've already mentioned. My friend said, "You know, Al, I had a discussion with a client of mine in St. Louis recently and happened to mention this same article. I told him where and when it appeared and about the fact that it emphasizes saving time by leaving the initiative with the other person. You know what he said to me? He said, 'Send me a copy, will you?'"

person's responsibility to complete the project and then to recommend either the major alternatives to be considered or a complete plan. The decision on degree of initiative is generally best made face-to-face between boss and subordinate rather than by mail. The personal contact allows information to be exchanged and a clear decision to be made.

The amount of initiative taken by subordinates must, of course, be rewarded. Those subordinates who are able to complete only the minimal job routines should receive fewer rewards, or, if such behavior is actually disruptive to good performance in the organization, that person should be removed from the job. Firing is the capital punishment of employee relations and should be resorted to only when it is absolutely clear that the expectations about the work to be performed have been established correctly by the boss and are not fulfilled.

To summarize, if you want to get the monkeys off your back, you should:

- Define a good job, including completed staff work.

- Assign the degree of initiative expected, including the date for review or approval.

- Make decisions to act jointly and personally with subordinates.

- Reward subordinates for taking initiative.

Managing Meetings

Another important step in your system of time management is how you conduct meetings. I suggest that you review your methods and that you make improvements where needed. I've already indicated that there are certain kinds of issues which are best handled by meetings. The problem is not so much whether or not to have meetings; rather, it is when they are best used and how to make them effective. There are a number of practices which seem to improve the quality and effectiveness of meetings. The following are some suggestions.

Publish an agenda. This is another way of saying, "Define a good job." A clear list of the issues to be dealt with is a road map for participants to follow. In addition, having an agenda will help insure that the necessary resources and information are present, will give the chairperson an opportunity to consider the proper process to be used for each item, and will give members an opportunity to consider whether they want to attend the meeting.

Publish a written record of the meeting. Decisions are made, information is generated, and policies are initiated in meetings; unless there is a written record, such outcomes are frequently misinterpreted or forgotten. There is a psychological principle called the Zeigarnik Effect which says that people tend to remember goals which are not accomplished and to forget goals which have been accomplished. As a result, individuals or groups may experience a sense of failure because they overattend to things that haven't been done. On an individual level, this is why keeping a log or reviewing the accomplishment of one's annual goals is important. It keeps progress in perspective by reminding one of the things that have been done. On the group level, the minutes will also document progress.

This can be particularly important where a group is dealing with an ambiguous issue which takes more than one meeting to resolve. If progress is not summarized, group members will think, "Oh my gosh, we have spun our wheels here for a whole hour and haven't accomplished anything. And they want to have another meeting to do the same thing!" A progress summary will identify the movement that has taken place and enhance support for further effort.

Start the meeting on time. I have emphasized that a manager should reward desired behavior rather than trying to persuade people to change or to punish undesired behavior. If being at the meeting has value to participants, then delaying its start merely rewards people for being late and punishes people for coming on time.

A recent experience of mine may make this point clear. Not long ago I was asked to speak to a group in a city in the Southwest. There is an organization called The Executive Committee (TEC), started by a retired executive named Bob Nourse, which arranges groups of nine to twelve top executives who meet together once a month for a full day. Members pay a monthly fee to the local TEC organizer and meet to work with a specialist who is brought to the group for the occasion or to work on problems of concern to the group members. There are now TEC groups all over the country.

On this occasion I was to meet with the group to discuss the three types of organization described at the beginning of this book. I got to the city on Thursday night for the Friday meeting, checked into a motel, and received a call from the local TEC organizer. He said, "We will be meeting in the board room of the new public library. I'll pick you up at 7:45 in the morning, and we'll start the meeting at 8:30." I got up a little late the next morning, rushed downstairs to grab a cup of coffee and a roll, and was in front of the motel at 7:45. No organizer. At 8:00 he showed up and we drove to the library. "We start at 8:30?" I said. "That's right," he said.

I got my equipment set up and was ready at 8:30. Of the nine men in the group, one was present at that time. By 8:45 we had three. By 8:55 we had seven. "Let's start," I said to the organizer. "We can't," he replied. "Why not?" "They're not all here." Finally, at 9:15 the last man arrived, and I looked at the organizer. "Now?" "Yes." I said, "Maybe I'm mistaken. I thought this was a *management development group* and that these people were paying their money to learn better management methods." "They are," said the organizer. "Well, if I were a member of this group, I would have learned just now to come to this group late. If I come on time, I have to sit around and wait. If I come late, I get rewarded." Needless to say, the organizer was a little annoyed, but my guess is that the group starts on time these days.

Start the meeting on time, and you will be amazed that many people who say, "Gee, I don't know what it is about me, I never get places on time" will arrive promptly.

State the ending time at the outset. By having a time constraint, group members will work more efficiently. In addition, those people with fast time clocks will be particularly grateful because the meeting, which seems longer to them (more internal time passes), will have a known target for completion.

Preschedule regular meetings. If you have board meetings or management committee meetings or others which occur on a regular basis, it is important to fix the time and dates for them well in advance. Calling ad hoc meetings can be terribly frustrating to those who are busy and who manage their time on a tight schedule. It's far better to schedule meetings in advance and then cancel them if there are not enough agenda items to warrant the gathering.

Distribute printed matter in advance of the meeting. There is no reason to use meeting time to read printed or technical information. Reading is an individual, not a group, activity. Again, if you are chairperson, reward desired behavior by proceeding on the assumption that group members have read the information. Those who neglect such responsibility will soon get the message that it is unrewarding to attend the meeting without having prepared for it.

Control processes according to task requirements. Like the other things we've discussed, the processes used in a meeting depend upon the circumstances. Let's take some situations and suggest what works in each.

One task for a group is to generate ideas. Perhaps the group has a problem and wants to develop solutions to it. This kind of *idea-generation* task will benefit, first of all, by having as many people involved as possible. For such a group to be most productive it is necessary that everyone be busy at the same time. As mentioned in Chapter 8,[2] *nominal grouping* works nicely for this purpose. Just ask all group members to list, in writing, solutions to the problem during a brief period of time, say ten minutes, without talking to each other. Then you list the solutions on a flipchart by taking the top item from each person's list, in round-robin fashion, then the next item from each list and so on until all items are listed. If the group is large, you will want to break it down into subgroups during the listing stage. As leader, your responsibility is to control the process that goes on, not tell people what to write.

Another task for a committee is *judgment and evaluation*. If time is important, use Robert's Rules of Order. On the other hand, if accuracy of judgment is important, I'd suggest using a consensus decision in a rather small group of five or seven informed people. Direct the group to discuss the issues until a solution acceptable to everyone is found. Caution members not to vote or average or resort to some other short cut. Tell them not to "give in" only to reach agreement and not to argue for an individual position. Facts and logic, rather than argument, become the substance of the discussion. Again, the chair's role in this kind of group is to maintain interaction and to keep the discussion within the rules. In this case the chair controls process, not content.

A third task for a committee may be one in which the leader wants to *influence* the group in some way. In this case the leader controls both the process and the content of the discussion. To be most effective, the leader will need to enhance or create expectations of enhancement of group members' needs by accomplishing an objective. This involves finding out what people want and linking their needs to the accomplishment of what the leader wants. It is rarely accomplished by persuasion and argument.

Finally, the purpose of the meeting may be *to disseminate or exchange information.* In dissemination the process and content are controlled by the leader in a clear, one-direction communication. Where information exchange is important, the leader controls the process of interaction by making sure that all parties are heard.

In short, each task has a different structure that is right. You can review the agenda before you have a meeting and decide how each item should be handled.

Don't hold meetings in your office. Meetings are best held in meeting rooms where the necessary equipment and furnishings are available. I prefer an open office arrangement—secrecy suggests lack of trust—and closed, private meeting rooms. Then, when your work in the meeting is finished, you can leave and return to your desk or office. On the other hand, if you hold meetings in your office, you can't terminate the discussion as easily. It is awkward to tell everyone to leave, and you can't say, "I have to get back to my office."

Alert visitors in advance about how much time you have

to spend with them. If your time is budgeted and you have a limited amount to spend with a visitor, tell the person. In that way the visitor can adjust what she has to say in the time available and will not be offended when you terminate the discussion.

Don't hold meetings and eat at the same time. Breaking bread with someone is an important social occasion. Trying to hold a meeting and eat at the same time not only reduces the social value, but it also is generally inefficient and upsetting physically. Ideally, I'd suggest eating together in a suitable place and then moving to a meeting room for work. Each physical environment is designed for a purpose; meeting rooms have appropriate facilities—visual aids, suitable furniture, no distracting sights or sounds, proper spatial arrangement, and, sometimes, a smoke precipitator. If you have to work and eat at the same location, at least finish eating as the first step and then change to work roles.

Handling Correspondence
The next few suggestions have to do with saving time in your correspondence. Somehow the whole process of correspondence seems to have undergone what some call a "means-ends conversion." That is, for some executives the correspondence process, which is supposed to be a means directed to the objective of communication with others, has become inverted so that the process has become an end in itself. It has become like the Changing of the Guard at Buckingham Palace. It is full of pomp and ritual. Here's how it seems to go for some people: Ms. Executive decides that she's going to handle some correspondence. First, she goes through the necessary ablutions. She clears her desk. She arranges her dictation machine. She goes to the bathroom, lights a cigarette, and then settles herself properly in her chair. Then she starts to dictate. Letters are answered, memos are written, with style and grace. Next she gives the tapes to her secretary. "Here is my correspondence," she says. "Good girl," says her secretary.

Now the secretary starts to type. Names and places have not been spelled, and some of her words are not clear. So, the secretary types a draft of the correspondence for the boss to edit and correct. The executive gets the drafts, corrects the spelling, and fills in the blanks, and then she returns them to the secretary. The secretary now does the official typing and places the letters and envelopes back on the executive's desk. In an elaborate pageant, the letters are lined up on the desk in a display of orderliness.

Now the executive begins the job of quality control for her secretary! She rereads everything, perhaps returning items that need correction and signs her name with a flourish. She folds each document neatly and places the items in the outgoing mail. "It's all finished," she tells her secretary. "Good girl," says the secretary.

If this pretty well applies to you and you enjoy the process, I won't knock it. If you want to save time and money, however, I'd like to suggest some tips which lack the style of this method but which will conserve time and energy.

Use handwritten messages to others. Three-layered carboned or carbonless interoffice memos are available in any office supply store. You write your message and keep the first copy. The respondent replies on the same form, keeping the second copy. You receive the final copy with your original message and the respondent's reply. The message gets through without a lot of pageantry.

Write short replies on original letters and return to the sender. It is common practice for some managers to make a handwritten reply on letters they receive, make a photocopy for their own files, and send the original back to the sender. This way both the message and response are on the same document; the objectives of communication are met.

Use form letters for standard correspondence. Standard items should be contained in a folder to be referred to by symbol for the secretary. The process needn't be impersonal since the memory typewriters now on the market permit you to address the letter personally and even to add a few additional sentences without composing the entire letter each time.

Don't reread and sign your correspondence. There is no point in doing quality control work for your secretary. You probably know about how many errors she makes right now. If you review her efforts, you are doing that person's work. Your time is more expensive than your secretary's.

Open second and third class mail once a week. By definition, second and third class mail has less urgency than first class mail. I'd suggest bunching the task of opening such mail and doing that job at the low ebb of your energy during the week.

Other Tips for Saving Time and Getting More from a Day

The previous discussion has dealt with major steps in a system of time management. In addition, there are a variety of techniques which different individuals have found to be useful. I include them here as tips, mainly because some people will choose to use them while others will feel that they aren't consistent with their own preference or style. You'll know which are appropriate for you.

To avoid procrastination, start with the least desirable task first. Champion, U.S. Olympic-type procrastinators seem to be able to use as much as a full day without ever getting to an undesirable task. If you are such a person, I'd suggest that you start with the task you really don't like, providing it is consistent with your general priorities for that day. In addition, if you need further help with this discipline, then you should also identify the reward that you will give yourself once you complete the least desirable task. One such reward can be a pleasant task. In learning theory this is known as the Premack Principle. Without ever knowing this, every parent practices the Premack Principle anyway when, for example, the parent says to a child, "You can't go out and play until you clean up your room."

To avoid procrastination, make sure that what is started is completed. Procrastinators are good at shuffling papers. For example, Mr. P enters the office, glances at his desk, and sees a letter that he hasn't answered. He picks it up and starts to read it but—Lo and Behold—beneath it is an article that he meant to review. Down goes the letter, up comes the article, and what do you know, beneath the article is a partially finished sales forecast. Up comes the sales forecast and, you guessed it, there is something else to attend to.

To avoid this pattern, discipline yourself so that if you pick up something and attend to it you will complete whatever is required. Two things will happen. First, you won't pick up as many things from your desk. Second, you won't have a lot of half-finished business lying around.

Use a tape recorder to fill unused time. Tape recorders can be used in a couple of ways. For one thing, you can do your dictation when you are sitting in an airport or riding in a car. Equally useful, you can listen to prerecorded tapes. The market is now flooded with prerecorded cassettes on a whole variety of subjects. Popular books, interviewing techniques, management by objectives, financial analysis, and many other topics are available. Some are great; some are terrible. In addition, they are expensive because they are easily duplicated. To conserve your own time and money, you might get your local Chamber of Commerce, public library, management club, or other group to buy them cooperatively and prescreen them. If you don't know where to find them, start by contacting the American Management Association, the American Society for Training and Development, or your local bookstore.

Use conference calls instead of meetings. If you have meetings with people outside your immediate geographic area that require them to travel to your location, and if the content of the meetings is essentially consultation or information giving, then try using conference calls for the same purpose. The telephone company will prearrange the telephone meeting, and the cost in time and money can be substantially less than your present arrangement. Or, you can purchase in-house systems which permit you to dial your own conference call.

Outline phone messages before making a call. In other words, define a good job. If you have ever placed a telephone call, carried on a conversation, hung up, and realized that you didn't cover the points that you called to discuss, try this tip. A few words written down will serve as a checklist and a reminder.

Follow a vigorous exercise program. There is a magic medicine available which will give you more energy, more productive hours, more emotional stamina, more alertness, and more resistance to the physical problems of aging. It's exercise. Exercise is not just for athletes; it's for everyone. There is a virtual supermarket of alternative forms; try them and find the one that you enjoy. Some managers go to early morning exercise classes at the YMCA–YWCA. Others jog, swim, or do yoga. Some play handball or tennis. The appropriate amount depends upon your present physical condition. Whatever exercise you choose should take place daily or several times a week and should be enjoyable.

Where work is scheduled on the basis of accomplishment rather than hours, employers would be well advised to provide time for employees to exercise, whether or not during conventional working hours. Productive time will be returned with a bonus for the hours invested in exercise.

Follow an active centering program. Meditation programs are not just for mystics; they are now widely accepted as a means for increasing concentration, reducing tension, and providing more energy. Have you ever finished a day and felt like you spent the whole time jumping from one thing to another, never finishing anything? Or, have you ever tried to concentrate on a problem only to find that your mind drifts to other things? Or, have you tried to reduce the pressure of work by using booze? If you've found yourself in any of these situations, try meditation.

As with exercise, there are lots of alternative forms of meditation available to you; just try several until you find one that you like. The basic forms generally ask you to sit comfortably in a quiet place and then free your mind of any thought, focus your attention on some object (flower, symbol, etc.), or repeat a word or phrase. All three will work, but one may be easier for some people than for others. Some systems are highly ritualized and mystical. Such methods tell you to sit in the lotus position, hold your hands in a particular way, etc. Less involved but equally effective methods say to sit comfortably, relax, and practice the recommended technique.

I'd also be wary of systems that cost a lot of money. Some of the meditation methods being sold these days remind me of encyclopedia deals. The product is good, but the cost and high-pressure sales gimmicks are unnecessary.

If you don't know where to start, check the phone book for a local meditation society (Yoga, Zen, or Transcendental), ask about classes in a bookstore selling books on the subject, or ask your minister or physician.

This completes the discussion of time management. You can judge whether I have done a good job in these chapters as I defined a good job for this sequence at the outset of Chapter 10. Once you have an understanding of your internal and external patterns of time use, you can employ the methods which we have described to design your own program of time management.

Chapter 12 Designing Your Organization — Two Structures

Did you ever feel like the whole world was a tuxedo and you were a pair of brown shoes?

George Gobel

The Romantic Way and the Classic Way

Up to this point I've been talking pretty much about you and your behavior. Now I want to focus on a broader view—how you might choose to organize your company or your part of a company. In doing this I must discuss the underlying logic of organization. Once this logic is clear, the details are easy to apply.

My understanding of organization design has been aided by a book which is not about organizations at all. The book has the curious title *Zen and the Art of Motorcycle Maintenance,* and its author is Robert Pirsig.[1] According to Pirsig there are two ways of looking at the world: the *romantic way* and the *classic way.* The romantic person looks at things from the outside. He has an aesthetic, artistic approach to things, is impressed by beauty and appearance, and is opposed to or mystified by technology. Such a person relies on others to make judgments within their specialties and goes to experts or professionals for service or advice.

In contrast, the classic person is concerned with how things work and how they are put together. She expects that if the process or thing can be understood, it can be changed or repaired or maintained by herself. The classic person sees beauty and usefulness in technology. She looks inside the thing being considered and, armed with this understanding, she will use specialists or professionals as sources of information rather than having them make decisions for her.

Pirsig also says that the apparent split between the romantic and the classic view of things is resolved once we realize how much of our perception is restricted by what we are taught to see by our culture or our environment. Left to ourselves, says Pirsig, we have a natural sense of what is right and what works. That sense of the correctness of things he describes as our natural awareness of quality.

All this may seem pretty remote from the subject of organization design, but I don't think so. It seems to me that most people who have been writing about organization generally have been romantic in their view. They take snapshots of organizations, describing their shape and size and the number of people reporting to the president, and so on, without really knowing what is going on inside. Very soon such descriptions get translated into prescriptions, and that's when the trouble starts. For example, romantic students of organization took snapshots of lots of enterprises and found that generally each person reported to only one boss. They probably had a few snapshots of people reporting to more than one boss, too, but these were discarded as inappropriate. Then, apparently, some of the people taking pictures of organizations stopped saying, "These pictures show people reporting to one boss" and started saying, "Each person *should* have only one boss." They became Experts and started giving Advice.

If those people interested in organizations had taken a classic view they might have asked, "Why do some people report to one boss while others report to several?" Had they done so, they would have found that having one boss merely simplifies the flow of communication, clarifies who evaluates and rewards whose work, and avoids confusing and conflicting directions from several people. If these problems can be overcome, there is no particular reason why a person can't have two or four or ten bosses. One boss is merely a convenience under some circumstances.

Fortunately, a classic view of organization is beginning to emerge. Research on organization structure is starting to ask questions about "how" and "why," so the underlying logic is far more clear now. With this information you can design your structure to meet your own needs.

Two Patterns of Organization
Let's go back to Pirsig's point that people left to themselves have a natural sense of what is appropriate. Most organizations that exist today were not designed by organization experts. Rather they just "happened," and as they evolved some person or persons made judgments about how the work was to be arranged. You can see an organization emerge if you give three people an assembly task to do. If there are several parts to be assembled, one of two basic patterns of organization is likely to emerge. In some cases the three people will divide all of the parts into three stacks, and each

person will make a complete assembly. In other cases, each will take part of the tasks so that a small assembly line develops. Both arrangements could be equally productive unless problems of materials develop, boredom occurs, the items being assembled are changed, or new people replace the old ones. Thus we see two basic types of organization which naturally emerge.

Consequences of these Arrangements

Now let's consider some of the consequences of the two arrangements. First, there is likely to be a shift from thinking about the work arrangement as something that *is,* to thinking about it as something that *should be.* If you remove one of the three workers and replace the person with another, what happens? The two workers show the new person how to do the task as it was previously arranged. The new person is told, "This is the way we do things here."

Second, the persons doing the whole task have a complete job to do. It has a beginning and an ending and contains a variety of substeps. On the other hand, people doing the assembly line task only have part of the job to do and they repeat a few steps over and over. It's likely that the whole-task people will understand the complete task better than the part-task people. It's also likely that the whole-task people will be better able to change the assembly if conditions or materials change. Altering the job in the assembly line requires more complicated rearranging of the work system. It may not seem natural, either, to the assembly line people to have their work changed.

Third, it's a whole lot easier to replace someone in the assembly line arrangement than in the whole-task arrangement. The work system is fixed in the assembly line, and the person learns only a few tasks. The whole-task arrangement is more complicated and more changeable; replacing someone requires more instruction and greater understanding from the new person.

There are lots of other considerations in this situation, too, such as the effect of different worker abilities, the need to balance the assembly line, the effects of increasing the number of people involved, but I'll save these for a later discussion in a different context. My point here is simply that correct organizations can and do emerge without any influence by an outside expert or even much conscious planning by those involved, but these quality structures can get stuck when *is* becomes *should be*. That's the means-ends conversion again. To avoid such dangers, you as a classic organization designer have to be able to understand how organizations operate. Such a view allows you to know when things need to be changed and what the consequences will be.

Understanding How Organizations Operate

The Bases for Survival
To do this, you need to understand what organizations do and which designs are appropriate for different purposes. Let's start with the bases for organization survival. There are at least three bases for survival. The first is being able to compete with others through efficient use of resources. This is the least cost and efficiency objective. It rests on the assumption that if there are several suppliers of a product and each provides the same quality, the consumers of the product will select the least expensive. The manufacture of plastic bags for dry cleaning establishments might be an example.

The second basis for survival involves the successful completion of a project. This is the one-of-a-kind type of job. Success depends upon whether or not it works and, often, completion within some kind of time constraint. An example of this type is a project to put a satellite in a particular orbit around the earth or to construct a building.

The third basis for survival is the ability to adapt products or services to varying needs of organization clients. Manufacturers of this sort produce by the unit or in small batches of the product, varying the product according to consumer requirements. Examples here are job shops or producers of fashion merchandise. The utility of the product to the customer, rather than least cost, becomes the necessary requirement.

Now consider the way in which the three types of organizations just indicated will deal with their consumers. The first will try to simplify consumer requirements so that a standardized product can be produced in high volume. We would expect that the work *system* involved would be relatively fixed for long periods of time. In contrast, the second and third types would be expected to alter their work systems as project or customer requirements change. Similarly, the skill level of people working in the standardized situation would be less than that of people working in new or varying product situations. If factors of size were not involved, the first type would be like the work arrangement described earlier in this chapter as an assembly line, while the second and third types would be more like the whole-task arrangement.

Some writers on organization have referred to the basic production process as the "technological core" of the organization.[2] Such writers point out that the structure of the organization depends upon the extent to which it can seal off the technological core and whether the technological core must react to and accommodate demands from outside the organization. To the extent that it can seal off its technological core, the organization and its work system are structured and formal and therefore are efficient. When it must be responsive to the environment, the organization is less structured and more informal.

Now let's go one more step with this discussion. We've just said that if the organization can seal off its operations from client demands, it can become formalized, structured, and efficient. It is relatively unresponsive to clients, instead acting upon its environment. Suppose that the organization has a virtual monopoly for its product or service. Can it seal off its processes and say "Take it or leave it" to its clients? You bet your boots! Suppose, further, that the organization provides a product to clients but does not depend upon the collection of money from clients for its survival. Can it say "Take it or leave it" to its clients? Sure. This situation explains why public monopolies like the telephone company, the local utility, or the post office seem so formal and impersonal.

Classification by Task: C- and E-Tasks
Where organizations must compete with each other for income from clients, their designs are strongly affected by the kind of technology involved and by size considerations. The issue of technology is well illustrated in a series of experiments by K. D. Mackenzie.[3] The nice thing about laboratory experiments is that they can reduce the complexity of the real world so that little pieces of it can be studied in depth. Mackenzie gave five-person groups two different tasks and observed what kind of organization was successful or unsuccessful with each.

The first kind of task required the application of a set of rules and a correct sequence of deductions. We'll call this the E-task. The second task required the generation and consideration of a variety of elements and inference of a correct solution rather than the application of a set of rules. We'll call this the C-task. The results showed that the E-task groups which were successful developed a centralized communication network with a leader. Once the leader and routines were established, the structure operated with efficiency.

In contrast, the C-task groups were successful if they did not develop a centralized, structured work arrangement. The successful C-task groups did not differentiate between the jobs of each member or the job of leadership. They worked as a group with equal member status and power and, as a result, produced more creative ideas. These studies suggest that where the need is for efficiency, the proper organization is one which is structured, explicit, and routine. Organizations performing E-tasks, then, are formalized. In contrast, where there is a need for creativity and adaptability, the proper organization is one in which people work as equal, undifferentiated members of a team. C-tasks require informal groups.

The next step in our development of the logic for organizing requires that we look at the issue of size in relation to basic strategies of organization. If we took snapshots of all kinds of organizations, businesses, government agencies, universities, hospitals, or whatever, we would find that among all kinds of enterprise there are only two basic strategies of organizing. That is, if we take a group of people, say 100, we have only two ways to structure them.

Looking at business enterprises, we would find that some had all of the people or equipment doing the same thing located in the same department. This is called a *functional structure.* In a business this might mean departments of sales, manufacturing, engineering, finance, and personnel. In contrast, we would find that in other businesses the larger structure would be divided into little businesses which are more or less independent of each other. In this case we might find that the major divisions of the company were identified by products (Product A Division and Product B Division) or by geographic areas (East Coast Division and West Coast Division). These divisions might be relatively small, and each would contain its own functional requirements for sales, manufacturing, engineering, finance, and personnel.

In the same way, looking at a research organization, we might expect to find each basic design. In a functional structure each department would contain all of the people doing the same kind of work, say data processing, systems analysis, engineering, or design. The alternative structure might be used with the whole research organization divided into projects. Each project might contain someone from data processing, systems analysis, engineering, and design.*

We have suggested that the basis for survival in some organizations is efficiency in order to compete on a cost-effective basis. Such organizations will perform E-type tasks if they are effective, and E-type tasks require clear structures and a set of clearly defined work rules. In contrast, where the organization survives on the basis of project completion or by serving a wide variety of clients on a made-to-order basis, it is

---

*Actually, there is a third type, a hybrid organization called a matrix. In a matrix structure each person in the research organization might have two unit affiliations and two bosses. For example, the members of the engineering department would be assigned temporarily to a project, reporting to the head of the engineering department and to the project leader. This structure is generally limited to very large organizations and will not be discussed in this book.

competing on the basis of creativity. Such organizations will perform C-type tasks if they are effective, and C-type tasks require people to work in rather informal teams.

Some readers will doubtlessly object to my emphasis on efficiency versus creativity, arguing that price is very important in firms dealing on a made-to-order basis or that customer service is vital for firms competing on a price-efficiency basis. An alternative way of looking at all this would be to picture the composition of the work force, the length of production runs, and the basis for achieving a sound return on investment.

In this alternative explanation, we may consider the efficiency organization as one in which the demand is fairly predictable, the production runs are relatively long (or at least repetitive), the workers are easily trained, and scheduling is tight. Typically, when size permits, specialized staff people will be present for production scheduling, inventory control, inspection, and other forms of internal control.

In contrast, the creative organization will have difficulty forecasting demand, production is by the piece or in small lots, the workers are skilled and hard to replace, and schedules are not as tight. Creative organizations will employ fewer specialized staff personnel simply because the systems and skills are held by the workers themselves.

This same basic distinction may be seen in retailing as well. Fast food services like hamburger chains are highly organized and efficient. Personnel may be replaced without serious disruption to the system. On the other hand, a gourmet restaurant will depend heavily upon the quality of its personnel and their loss can be serious to the enterprise.

The relative emphasis upon efficiency or a made-to-order technology shows up in pricing policy. In the efficiency firm, the return on investment depends upon a relatively small ratio of income to sales and a highly efficient use of assets employed. In contrast, the made-to-order technology will have higher income to sales ratio but a smaller capital turnover. Within these limits, then, the efficiency firm must organize tightly, and the made-to-order firm must organize in a way which gives the service or creativity that its customers expect of it.

Classification by Structure

The next step in our understanding and use of organization design is to identify its two basic forms: (a) functional and (b) goal-oriented or team. To be a functional organization the company or its departments must have two things: (1) people doing the same jobs organized in the same department, and (2) enough personnel in the department for people to identify with their job, skill, or professional group, not the larger organization. My guess is that a minimum of five or six people will bring about the latter. Thus, in Figure 6 (page 160) each functional department (sales, production, and engineering) has a grouping by job type and has enough people to cause identification with the department. In addition, it is properly matched with its survival goal and groups performing E-type tasks.

The second type of organization design is called goal-oriented or team. This structure has a mixture of skills working together on a goal or project as a team. The goal-oriented units may be two small product divisions, as indicated in Figure 6, or they may be project groups or two small plants in different geographic areas. In addition, they are properly matched with survival goals of service or creativity, and they perform C-type tasks.

Now, let's take some examples of alternative organization designs. Within an organization, the use of a secretarial pool is a functional organization designed for efficiency. An alternative, using private secretaries, would be a goal-oriented design; the manager and the secretary would be a team.

In the same way, looking at a research organization, we might find departments of data processing, systems analysis, engineering, and design, with enough people in each to be a functional organization. Or, the same group of people might be organized into project groups, each with its own data processing, systems, engineering, and design people working as teams.

Similarly, we might find a large retailer selling, among other things, paint and hardware. If you were to go into the

Figure 6. Example of a Functional and a Goal-Oriented Structure

Survival Basis: Efficiency   Service; Creativity
Task: E-Type   C-Type
Organization: Functional   Goal-Oriented or Team

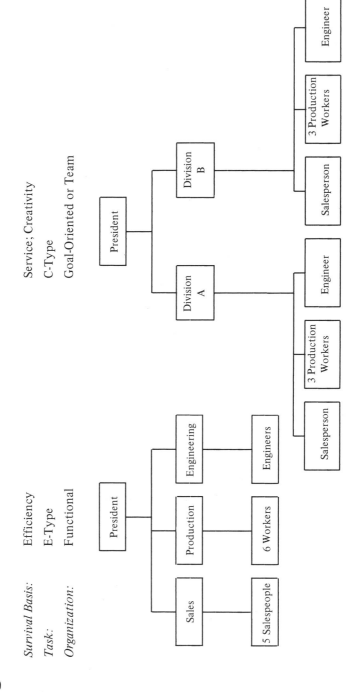

paint department, you might say to one of the people there, "Say, I have paint peeling off the side of my house. Would you mind coming over to see what the trouble might be?" The response might well be: "Look, mister, we sell good paint here and the price is reasonable. We don't go driving around to look at people's houses!" In contrast, suppose that you go to the local home decorating center in your neighborhood. In response to the same question, the person working there might say, "Sure, will this afternoon be OK?" Will this service be expensive? Certainly. Will it be good? It had better be.

Later in this chapter I will show what happens as the functional and goal-oriented organizations get bigger. For the present, let's consider why each operates the way it does.

Characteristics of Functional Organizations
Now let's consider the usual characteristics of functional structures which are large enough to permit the use of several people doing the same work in the same department.[4]

Development of subspecialties. By having several people doing the same work in the same department, it becomes possible to develop subspecialties. For example, one person in the typing pool might specialize on correspondence, while another works on technical reports, and a third works on standardized promotion letters. Or, an engineering department might have an electromechanical and electronics engineer.

Advancement in specialty. Where specialists are grouped together, it becomes possible to advance people within their specialty. Thus the typists might advance from typist Grade I to typist Grade II.

Supervision by a specialist. The heads of functional departments are likely to be specialists in the area managed and thus can evaluate the technical or professional performance of those supervised.

Professional contagion. By working with others engaged in the same type of work, each person has an opportunity to gain additional skill from others.

Maximum use of resources. The addition of personnel or

equipment in a functional department is likely to be based upon a demonstration of full-time utilization of the resource. For example, a new typist will be added to the typing pool when it can be demonstrated that the person can be kept busy full time. In contrast, in the goal-oriented structure an executive merely argues that she needs a secretary because some secretarial needs will occur from time to time.

Difficulty in coordinating and scheduling. When a functional organization contains several functional departments which are large enough to have several specialists of the same type in each that are dependent upon each other, coordinating and scheduling become big problems. For example, if the company with the typing pool also has a sales department, an engineering department, and a manufacturing department, keeping things in balance is difficult. Suppose that sales orders are typed in the typing pool and sent to manufacturing and engineering. Keeping the work flow balanced between the four departments can be a real problem. Or, suppose the production process itself has a group of drill presses in one department, paint processes in another department, and packaging in a third. If orders for lots of products are coming in, it becomes difficult to coordinate the work of the three departments.

Conflict between departments. Given the difficulties of scheduling between departments which are interdependent, conflict is likely to occur. One typical conflict is between sales and manufacturing. The sales people say, "If those people in manufacturing would get to work and meet their responsibilities, we wouldn't have customers on our back all the time, complaining about their orders being late." In contrast, the manufacturing people say, "If you guys would stop making unrealistic promises about delivery dates, we could get the stuff out on time."

Formal organization. As I've already pointed out, functional structures are more likely than goal-oriented structures to have formal rules, formal reporting relationships, and fixed goals and procedures. This formality means that the organization will be relatively inflexible and hard to change.

Short time perspective. There is some evidence that

people in functional organizations are likely to take a short-run perspective of things. If the work is routine, people will see what has to be done today rather than look to the end of completing the product and delivering it to the consumer. On the other hand, a goal-oriented structure, such as a home building project, is more likely to take a longer-range view of things, considering the whole process of construction and the final completion date.

Characteristics of Goal-Oriented Organizations
Goal-oriented structures have the opposite characteristics. Here are some of them.

Lack of specialization. Where the organization has one or more relatively small, mixed-skill groups organized on the basis of product, type of customer, geographic area, or projects, subspecialties can't develop and each specialist is expected to have a high level of talent. In the typing pool example of a functional organization, it is possible to employ new people at a low level of skill and then to advance them in the typing pool as they gain experience. On the other hand, a single secretary serving an executive must be able to do everything necessary in the job.

Supervision by a manager, not a specialist. In goal-oriented organizations, the head of the unit or department cannot be a specialist in all areas and must be a professional manager instead. For example, the project leader in a research and development division may have data processing, systems, engineering, and design people under his control. He is less able to evaluate their technical ability than a specialist in each function would be, so he must rely more upon managerial than technical ability to get the work done. This characteristic of a goal-oriented structure can be an advantage since it can provide a training ground for administrators in the company.

Low in professional contagion. Goal-oriented structures don't provide much professional contagion for their specialists. If all the engineers are assigned to one department, they can learn new skills from each other. On the other hand, if each engineer is assigned to a different project, lack of contact between the engineers prevents such learning from happening.

Tendency toward smallness and flexibility. Goal-oriented structures tend to be small, relatively informal groups of different specialties which are independent of each other and which focus more on the project goal or the client need. They are likely to be creative and flexible, and to take a longer time perspective. It should be clear by this time that since they duplicate resources and operate with personal, informal processes, they are less efficient compared with functional structures but better able to solve problems or meet varied client needs.

Usefulness of Each Type
The relative usefulness of the two organizations, then, depends upon the earlier mentioned survival needs of the organization. Where the organization is concerned primarily with cost and price efficiency, the functional structure is probably best. On the other hand, where the survival of the organization depends upon being able to meet client needs or complete a project, and where efficiency is not the primary consideration, the goal-oriented structure is probably the best.

Changes in the Organization
We are now ready to answer some basic questions about changes in organizations. The answers should be clear from what we have said already.

What happens as a goal-oriented organization gets larger? Let's take an example. Suppose that you and a couple of friends start a small advertising agency. You plan to work together closely, handling a variety of functions like selling, design, editing, etc. You get your first customer. That person gets all kinds of service from your team. Your reputation spreads and your company grows. The service is still excellent. Finally, one day the agency is large enough to have five or more people each in the editorial department, the sales department, the art department, the design department, and so on.

Now Mr. Smith, who has a large advertising campaign in the works, calls you and says, "Hello, this is Smith, how's my ad campaign coming?" You say, "Who?" Smith says, "Don't you know me?" You say, "Listen, I think that you had better call the sales department; here is the number . . . ."

Smith calls sales. "Hello," he says, "this is Mr. Smith. How is my campaign coming?" "Who?" says the sales manager. "Smith." "Say," says the sales manager, "Why don't you call the art department. Here is the number . . . ."

What has happened here? A goal-oriented structure has grown into a functional organization without anyone knowing it. Its survival is based on creativity and service, but it now has people performing E-type tasks in a functional organization designed for efficiency, not service.

What should the company do? It should reorganize. It may employ account representatives to handle big accounts or several small ones. It may establish a customer service department to keep track of projects. It may create several smaller agencies to serve different parts of the country. It may restrict its size. Or, it may change its goals to serve a part of the advertising market which requires routine processing on a price-competitive basis instead of creativity.

What happens when a company whose survival goals depend upon efficiency gets larger? Suppose that you are now a small manufacturer of stock cardboard cartons. You are competing with a variety of large companies whose product is essentially the same as yours, and efficiency and price are essential. You don't really have enough people to have a functional organization, but with enough effort you may be able to get by—if you minimize your overhead and put in a lot of hours yourself. Suppose the company grows. What will happen? If you establish the proper controls for efficiency, everything gets better and better. You can subdivide the labor. You can employ inexpensive labor and train your own people. You can improve on your equipment and use more single-purpose machinery. Your departments are run by specialists in each function. You will get better control over sources of supply. Eventually, you will employ specialists to provide control over quality, costing, inventory, scheduling, budgeting, and performance appraisal. And, as things get better and better, you will wonder how you ever made it as a small shop.

What happens if a creative project comes up in a functional structure? To continue the previous example, suppose that you learn that someone in Europe has developed a plastic substitute for cardboard that costs a fraction of your present raw material. Are you going to wait around to see whether this is true? Hardly. You may choose to drop everything and study the situation yourself. The disadvantages with this are that the company may need you and you may not have enough varied technical knowledge to handle the problems. Another alternative would be to ask the heads of your functional departments to study the situation and send you a report. Chances are you would end up with five reports which don't fit together.

Since this is a C-type task, perhaps the best strategy would be to form a project group with appropriate people from each of your departments. You might well say, "Folks, you have exactly thirty days to give me a feasibility study of the application of this new material to our processes and market." If they say, "Can we have a secretary or travel money?" my guess is that you would say, "I'm not talking about economy; I'm interested in the survival of our company. Get me the report in thirty days."

Doesn't every organization have some departments or units which perform C-type tasks and some that perform E-type tasks? Of course it does. The company will have a pretty clear basis for survival, but the departments in it are designed for different purposes. By standardizing the operations in departments where you want efficiency, you can employ the energy, money, and creativity required for service or projects where it is best used. By listing the various departments in your company under two headings—service and efficiency—you will see which should be standardized and which should be teams of people. One team which will exist in every functional organization is the one involving you and the functional department heads. That one should meet regularly to plan for the future and to solve problems creatively.

What happens if a company clearly has two goals—one product line with high volume and a price-competitive market; the other a job-shop technology? The first thing to do is to find out whether you are making an adequate return on investment in both. Often, the profits on one go to pay for the losses on the other. This may occur if the same people are performing both kinds of work. You may plan on physically separating the two operations when economy permits. They are entirely different kinds of organizations and people, and they will grate on each other if they are together.

Summary
I'll have more to say about organization design in your own company in the next chapter. For the present, let's summarize by suggesting that if you as a manager wish to increase the appropriateness of your organization structure, you should do the following:

• Avoid copying someone else's organization structure unless you are sure that *what is* is also *what should be.*

• Determine whether the basis of your company survival is cost/price efficiency, successful project completion, or the provision of products or services on a made-to-order basis.

• Develop formal, structured work systems for routine E-type tasks.

• Develop group-centered, informal teams for creative C-type tasks.

• Develop functional organizations where the product demand is stable and production runs are relatively long or repetitive.

• Develop functional organizations where cost/price efficiency is the basis for survival or the objective.

• Develop goal-oriented organizations where the basis for survival or the objective is project completion or service.

• Shift from a functional to a goal-oriented structure

when the competitive situation or objectives change from efficiency to the need for service or creativity.

- Shift from a goal-oriented to a functional organization when the competitive situation or objectives change from creativity or service to cost/price efficiency.

Chapter 13 Designing Your Organization — Some Key Dimensions

When choosing between two evils, I always take one I haven't tried before.

Mae West, *Klondike Annie*

Organization by Evolution or by Design

In the last chapter I suggested that if people have a job to do that requires joint effort, they will eventually arrange themselves into some kind of organization without conscious planning. This is probably the way most companies develop their structure. A few people work together and some kind of work arrangement develops, based on their talents, preferences, and previous experience. As more people are added, the organization evolves with little thought about the work arrangements. As noted in Chapter 5, this kind of structure is based heavily upon the type of people involved, and many employees are likely to be considered as indispensable.

There is also a second way to get organized; it is based upon conscious planning. In such cases the chief executive or someone else tries to arrange the work system in a way that meets the needs of both the company and the employees. This second method develops a work arrangement in which individuals are less likely to be considered indispensable.

My experience indicates that craft and promotion companies are more likely to use the first approach. They let the organization just happen. In contrast, administrative types are more likely to plan their work arrangements according to the objectives of the company and the needs of the people included. As I will show in this chapter, the type of administrative structure that is appropriate will depend upon the size and technology of the firm. We need to determine what works when.

My understanding of what kind of organization is best under different conditions has been helped enormously by the work of Jay Galbraith[1] at the University of Pennsylvania. Galbraith suggests that we think of an organization as a device which processes information. In general, the more uncertainty there is, the greater will be the amount of information processing.

For example, consider the simple task of getting to work at a place of employment. Let's suppose that you have been newly hired by a company in a different city and that you are temporarily staying in a hotel while you get established in the new location. Your task is to arrive at the company at the proper time and report to your new boss. You must consider what time is proper, the appropriate clothes to wear, the company's exact location, and the route to it. Decisions must be made about the form of transportation, the time of travel, and the cost involved. Finding the new employer's office may require directions; communicating with him before arriving may be required. Clearly, you must process a relatively large amount of information because of the uncertainty in the situation. As this uncertainty is reduced, the information processing will also be less. To the extent that you are given maps, rules, standards, and other clear information before you attempt the task, your information processing job is reduced. Similarly, to the extent that you acquire guidelines through experience, it is also simplified.

Conditions Influencing Amount of Information Processing

In any organization there are at least three main conditions which influence the amount of information which must be processed to insure effective performance. The first of these is the degree of uncertainty about what is required to do a task. The less clear the issues about the proper tooling, staffing, money, time, and the like, the more information that must be processed. The second condition is the number of elements involved in decision making. By elements I mean people, occupations, or organizational units. Thus it is more complicated for five people to make a decision than for one to do so. The third condition which influences the amount of information processing required is the degree of interdependence or interconnectedness between the elements involved in the task. One expects more information processing between departments in a functional structure where they rely upon performance from each other than between five project groups which do not depend upon each other for anything.

Major Steps for Organizing Information Processing

You may have an idea where this discussion is taking us, from what I have said so far. You may recall that rules—or traffic lights—will reduce the amount of information processing. Or, you may have recalled that C-type tasks require more information processing than E-type tasks. Or, you may have considered that as an organization gets larger, information processing requirements increase. If you have, you are on the right track. Now, I want to suggest what steps you can take to organize and to cope with information processing requirements in your company. The steps identified apply to any organization. My examples will focus on manufacturing, since that is where detailed information is available.

As Galbraith suggests, the first steps to be taken include (1) establishing rules, policies, and procedures, (2) identifying the structure, and (3) specifying goals or standards. Let's consider each in detail.

Establish Rules, Policies and Procedures
The presence of these guidelines makes it likely that activities will take place according to plans and that the different activities will fit together. By creating them intentionally rather than letting them evolve, it is more likely that they will be based upon needs for effectiveness.

I'd recommend that even small businesses develop a company policy manual for all of their managers. The value of such tools may be illustrated as follows: When I was a young college student, I remember taking a course in management in which we were shown the nicely printed policy manuals from some big corporations. It always seemed to me that the policies would say, "This company dedicates itself to producing a quality product at a fair price and to the service of our customers." I remember thinking that such statements had no meaning for me, and I doubted that they would have much influence on the people in the company either. More recently, as a partner in a small consulting firm, I realized that we three partners were always arguing about details after something took place. Our company manager would say, "Look, we've got to cut down on our expenses. We are all spending too much money when we travel." As a result, I would buy coach fare tickets on the plane and would take a taxi instead of renting a car. Then I found out that another partner was traveling first class and that an employee of the company continued to rent a car. Finally, the three of us sat down and developed a policy manual.

We agreed on the distribution of work and on our relative authority. We came to a consensus on the expenses which could be charged to the company. We agreed on our market and upon the activities which were not considered part of the company. We decided on prices and upon the contribution to company overhead. We continued to add to these policies as time passed. The result: no arguments and better coordination. Information processing was greatly reduced.

For this reason, I'd suggest that a company provide each of its managers with some kind of binder which permits adding or changing pages easily. An inexpensive three- or seven-ring notebook will do nicely. Then each manager should receive a set of policies, one policy to a page, and a table of contents. As policies are changed or added, each manager will get two pages: a new table of contents and the new or changed policy. Another alternative is to obtain a standard guide for policies such as that shown in Table 5[2] and adjust it to fit your own needs. A policy manual will reduce the amount of information processing and give you more time to spend on nonpredictable matters.

Policies have other advantages as well. They reduce the amount of discretionary action which managers may exercise with their subordinates. Thus, policies constrain capricious and arbitrary actions by a boss. A second effect, mentioned in Chapter 5, is that by being better able to predict each other's actions, people will have more felt freedom to act. Third, the presence of policies will increase the amount of decentralization which can take place since appropriate actions may be taken by people without the need to get personal approval from a boss.

The same logic applies to procedures. Where activities are fairly repetitive, it's a good idea to write them down in the form of procedures or checklists. This is easier in a functional organization where products and operations are relatively standardized. Even in goal-oriented structures, however, there are some repetitive routines which can be for-

Table 5. Example of Policy Guide†

Subject   VACATION POLICY

1. **POLICY**

    All employees (except temporary) shall be granted vacation with pay depending upon length of continuous employment as of January 1 of each year.

2. **QUALIFICATIONS**

    Employment for twelve (12) months or more but less than ten (10) years ------------
    2 calendar weeks

    Employment for ten (10) years but less than twenty-five (25) years -----------------
    3 calendar weeks

    Employment for twenty-five (25) years or more --------------------------------
    4 calendar weeks

    President and Vice Presidents ---
    1 month

    Others on confidential payroll --
    3 calendar weeks

3. **NEW EMPLOYEES**

    a. Employees hired during the first six (6) months of the year can take a one week vacation after six (6) months of employment, provided it can be taken in the same calendar year. These employees then receive two (2) weeks of vacation in the following calendar year after twelve (12) months of employment.

    b. Employees hired during the last six (6) months of the year receive two weeks of vacation in the following calendar year, after twelve (12) months of employment. They have the option of taking one of these weeks after six (6) months of employment.

4. **CARRY-OVER**

    Employees shall not be authorized to carry over any unused vacation time from one calendar year to another. Any unused vacation will be forfeited unless such vacation remains unused at the company's request, in which case disposition will be made by the company President.

Originally issued _____

Revised _____   *Page* _____ *of* _____

                Approved _____
                              President

†From *Company Policy Manual* by D. Van Beck. Champaign, IL: Research Press Co., 1978. Used with permission.

Table 5. Example of Policy Guide (continued)

Subject   VACATION POLICY (Continued)

5. **VACATION PAY**
   a. Unless otherwise directed by the employee, and approved by the manager, a payroll check will be issued on the last work day preceding start of vacation for time worked plus vacation allowance.
   b. Prior to leaving on vacation an employee will receive any check or checks which normally would have been distributed during the period of his vacation.

6. **PAYMENT IN LIEU OF VACATION**
   Since vacations are intended to provide rest and diversion from the regular work routine, payment in lieu of time off will not be granted.

7. **HOLIDAYS DURING VACATION**
   When a recognized holiday falls during a scheduled vacation period, an additional day off mutually agreed upon by the employee and the manager will be granted. This additional pay may be taken in advance if it is contiguous to the vacation. It need not be contiguous in which case it may be taken at a later time.

8. **SCHEDULING**
   a. Vacations shall be taken at a time mutually agreed upon by the employee and the manager. All other factors being equal, schedules will be arranged on the basis of the work load and employee (companywide) seniority.
   b. Vacation time will be taken in units of not less than one (1) full calendar week, and shall begin on the first day of the week. Vacations will not be scheduled to begin on the last Monday of December when it becomes impossible to complete a five (5) day vacation period within the same calendar year.

9. **TERMINATIONS**
   Any employee who has been employed for twelve (12) months or more shall be paid at time of termination for any unused vacation. In such cases, the effective date of termination will still be the last day worked.

10. **EMPLOYEES ON LESS-THAN-FULL-TIME OR TEMPORARY BASIS**
    a. Employees on regular less-than-full-time jobs shall receive vacation time proportionate to the average number of hours worked.
    b. Employees working on temporary jobs, either full-time or less-than-full-time, shall not be entitled to any vacation benefits.

11. **EXCEPTIONS**
    Any exceptions to this vacation policy, or to any of its provisions, shall be reported in writing to personnel and must carry the approval of the company President.

Originally issued _____
Revised _____   *Page* _____ *of* _____
                       Approved _____
                                President

malized to reduce information processing.

Identify the Structure

Another thing which every company can do to reduce the amount of information processing is to draw the organization structure as it exists now and to draw the ideal structure as well. Drawing and circulating the present structure will clarify channels of authority and information flow.

A clear structure is important for several reasons. First, it will identify reporting relationships so that each person knows to whom he reports. Every person in an organization needs to know who has a legitimate right to give him directions and who represents his needs and evaluates his work. I recently asked the president of a company to identify his subordinates. He mentioned five. I then interviewed the managers in the company, asking among other things the person to whom they reported. Nine people mentioned the president as their boss. Another number mentioned two or more people as their superiors. This pattern was costly because some managers complained that the president undermined their authority by bypassing them in his contacts with their subordinates; some employees made a practice of contacting the president directly. The preparation of the organization chart reduced this confusion.

The development of the present organization in chart form also will highlight any imbalances in responsibilities which exist. Some people on the same level and with the same pay may be shown to have vastly different levels of supervisory responsibility. Further, the formal statement of the organization will show illogical job titles or combinations of responsibilities. Finally, the chart will aid in identifying when a team structure is beginning to evolve into a functional organization. This often happens when the total company employment reaches a point at which the chief executive can no longer monitor the whole operation with informal methods.

The next step in organizing is to draw the ideal structure and make plans to implement it. Perhaps the first recorded statement about organization design comes from the Bible when Moses' father-in-law, Jethro, told him to stop trying to run the whole show himself and to utilize his middle managers. He said:

> Thou shalt provide out of all the people able men . . . to be rulers of thousands, rulers of hundreds, rulers of fifties, and rulers of tens; and let them judge the people at all seasons; and it shall be, that every great matter they shall bring unto thee, but every small matter they shall judge; so shall it be easier for thyself, and they shall bear the burden with thee.[3]

As you can see from this structure recommended by Jethro, you will have a couple of related problems in designing your organization: (1) How many levels should exist? and (2) How many people should report to each manager?

Before I answer those questions I want to emphasize that the organization exists *to do something.* The objective is not an organization structure; the objective is more productive and better satisfied people. It is a tool, not a picture to hang on the wall. As explained in Chapter 12, the classic approach to organization is one in which you understand parts of the organization and how they work. The romantic approach is to say, "I hired this expert to design my organization, and I bought that fancy display chart to hang it on the wall."

Let's start with the first problem about how many levels should exist in your organization. The best answer would be obtained by experimenting with your structure until you find the exact number of levels which meet your needs and the needs of others. Since this is impractical, the next best approach is to try to find out how many levels are too few and how many appear to be too many. With too many levels the organization spends more money on administrative expense than is necessary, and information must travel through more people than needed. With too few, managers will be overburdened with short-term matters, won't be able to deal with exceptions that arise, and won't coordinate the work of subordinates effectively. In other words, with too many there is excess capacity to process information; with too few there isn't enough capacity.

Studies of the number of levels show some consistency. One study [4] of 128 organizations indicated that they had about 4 levels with 100 employees, 6 levels with 1000 and between 7 and 8 levels with 10,000 employees. These are all levels including workers.

A study by Woodward [5] considered 100 manufacturing firms with more than 100 employees and divided these according to technology. Those with unit or small-batch production averaged three levels (A, B, and C in Figure 7, page 180) of management or four levels in all (A, B, C, and D in Figure 7). Those with large-batch or mass production had four levels of management or five levels in all.

My own investigation with Professor Ray Aldag[6] shows that unit or small-batch firms averaging forty-four employees had three levels of management and large-batch or mass-production firms averaging fifty-eight employees had nearly four levels of supervision.

If you vary from the number of levels indicated, you are not necessarily wrong. But you ought to think through the reason for the difference and whether other evidence tells you that you have too much or too little information-processing capacity. More precise information can be obtained by your trade association if it has conducted staffing surveys in your trade, broken down by size, technology, and measures of success.

The next question involves how many people should report to each manager. Figure 7 shows four B's reporting to A. Is this appropriate? How many D's should report to C? Again, there are trade-offs involved. If too many subordinates report to a supervisor, they suffer from too little direction and coordination; if too few are assigned to a manager, supervisory expense will be unnecessarily large.

The proper number is what works best for you. As with the number of levels, the experience of other firms can be helpful. In this case it appears that practices for the chief executive are less systematic than for supervisors. Chief executives seem to vary their reporting relationships to suit

Figure 7. Hypothetical Organization Structure

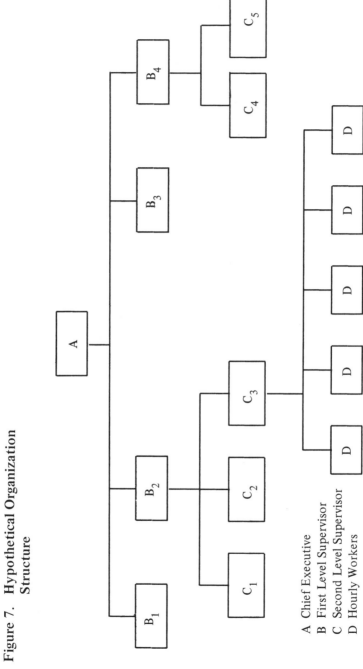

A Chief Executive
B First Level Supervisor
C Second Level Supervisor
D Hourly Workers

their style. Some may have only a general manager reporting to them. Others will have elaborate corporate staffs supporting their efforts. Some will have functional managers under their control.

Woodward found that in unit and small-batch production, an average of four people reported to the chief executive. In large-batch and mass production the average was seven. Rather than adhere to these numbers, you, as chief executive, should ask yourself what is *not* being accomplished if you have a relatively large number of people under your control. If you are caught up in day-to-day problems, perhaps planning for future needs is being sacrificed. In any case, your span of supervision should suit your style of operating.

When we consider the appropriate span of supervision at lower levels of management, the proper number of people to supervise varies more systematically. To understand why this is possible, let's look at conditions which may affect the ideal span of control for a manager.

Similarity of jobs supervised. The information processing requirements are less when supervising jobs which are the same than they are when supervising jobs which are different. More people can be supervised effectively when the jobs are similar.

Closeness of the jobs to each other. Information processing is more complex when people supervised are not physically close to each other. Where those supervised are in different locations, fewer can be supervised effectively.

Uniqueness of tasks involved. Where people are dealing with unique, nonrepetitive tasks, the information processing requirements generally require that fewer are supervised by a manager.

Amount of nonsupervisory work performed by managers. When managers do work similar to that of their subordinates or do some other kind of unrelated work, they can supervise fewer people effectively.

Relative competence of supervisor or subordinate. As might be expected, the ability of supervisors and subordinates will affect the ideal span of supervision. Viewed in another way, this means that employing talented people who require less supervision allows the organization to reduce its supervisory expense.

Degree of standardization of jobs supervised. As we have already indicated, by standardizing rules and procedures, the degree of information processing is reduced and supervisory expense is reduced.

Degree of supervisory assistance. The use of personal assistants, or partial supervision from others, such as staff people, can increase a supervisor's span of control.

Job design of people supervised. As I will discuss in the next chapter, when jobs are designed so that people have full responsibility for the work arrangement—completion of a whole job and control of work quality—they often require less supervision; one manager can direct more of these jobs than other types.

These characteristics help to explain why Woodward found that the span of control of first-line production supervisors averaged between twenty-one and thirty for small-batch firms and between forty-one and fifty for large-batch firms. Similarly, another study[7] found an average of twenty persons in unit production and twenty-five persons in large-batch production. Since large-batch firms are typically more routine and highly structured than small-batch firms, it is logical that supervisors in large-batch firms would oversee more subordinates effectively.

To determine whether you are understaffed or overstaffed either in terms of all employees or in terms of categories of employees (administration, for example), you can look at several sources of information.

Compare your own operation with that of other companies of a similar size if your trade association publishes staffing ratios. Staffing ratios also will help you determine when you can afford to hire a specialist or staff person. For example, a survey of automotive parts manufacturers done some years ago[8] indicated that on the average the companies employed a purchasing agent with sixty-three full-time production workers, a production planning and control person with seventy-five full-time workers, a personnel specialist with seventy-seven, and an accountant with forty-eight. These figures may not be useful to you, but they suggest the information that is possible to obtain.

Look at sales per employee and sales per administrative person historically and in comparison with other, similar companies. Again, your trade association should be giving you this information. For example, the Printing Industries of America Association and its Canadian equivalent, Graphic Arts Industries Association, publish detailed studies about the cost of doing business. In their 1976-77 report,[9] sales per all employees averaged $42,065 for U.S. firms and $38,910 for Canadian firms. Such figures also are available for a variety of other categories including sales per administrative employee, salesperson, and factory person. The figures are also available by size of company. Thus member organizations may get some specific information about whether or not they are overemployed or underemployed and about the relative efficiency of their companies compared with others. From a historical perspective I would expect sales per employee to increase as a company grows. If yours don't, you may be overemploying.

Compare your administrative expense categories with firms of similar size in your industry. You can obtain a quarterly report of income and expense in your industry from the *Quarterly Financial Report for Manufacturing Corporations,** published quarterly by the Federal Trade Commission.

Use your own good sense. Being different from others doesn't mean you are wrong. You may be doing something better than all the rest. All I would caution is that underemploying people, particularly managers and specialists, can reduce profits and growth as much as overemploying. As I've indicated before, specialists more than pay for themselves from the savings or income they generate if they are used properly.

There are other problems involved in identifying the structure besides the questions of levels and spans; we will

---

*Order from Superintendent of Documents, U.S. Government Printing Office, Washington, D.C. 20402. Price: $4.50 per year.

consider them shortly. They involve the choice of E-type or C-type departments, the use of boards or committees, and the big problem of job design. We'll get to these when we discuss increasing or decreasing the need for information processing in the company. At this point, however, let us consider establishment of performance standards.

Set Performance Standards
As an organization gets larger, it becomes increasingly important for decisions to be made where the action is. Otherwise, as the business gets larger, with more levels, the information processing will increase because more and more information must filter to the top of the structure for interpretation and decisions. An example may make this clear. I often ask company presidents, "How do you know what is happening in production?" In response, I generally get one of two kinds of answers. One president will say, "I spend a lot of time walking around the plant. You just sort of know when something isn't right. I mean, you can sense when something doesn't feel or sound right."

In the other response the president says, "I meet each Monday morning with my department heads to compare budgeted operations for the previous week with performance. Then we make plans for the coming week, adjusting budgets and plans if necessary." The first kind of president may be spending a lot of valuable time trying to stay on top of things informally. And, he may be bypassing people trained to do managing for him. Both actions can be costly. In contrast, the second president is *using a system* to run the organization in which middle managers are more likely to be exercising their own responsibility and authority.

Actually, two kinds of performance standards are needed. The first are *activity* goals. These are ongoing activities in the organization such as money spent, sales in units and dollars, scrap rates, absenteeism, or units produced. These ongoing activities need to be broken down by time periods. The time periods used depend upon your operation; they may be hourly, daily, weekly, or monthly. It's a good idea to chart income and expenses over time to follow trends and make adjustments. If you are really in the dark about where to start, I'd suggest that you take your present income statement and project it out for a year. Then see which departments are responsible for various items on the income statement and hold them accountable for standards set. I'd also suggest that you set standards for three levels of income: an optimistic level, an expected level, and a pessimistic level. It is possible to survive or make a profit in a terrible year, providing expenses are kept in line with income.

The second type of standard is a *project goal*. Projects are one-shot efforts like preparing a feasibility study, paving the parking lot, or having a dealer conference. The time, money, personnel, and activities of the project should be scheduled, but the most important part of setting project standards is to define the outcome in as much detail as possible. Both activity and project goals are forms of defining a good job. As I have said repeatedly, define a good job at the beginning and you will increase the degree to which goals will be accomplished.

If you are in large-batch or mass production or some other kind of organization which has standardized operations and meets a stable, predictable demand for products or services, you will want to do a lot of advanced planning of systems and procedures. Such plans include the scheduling of work through the plant, the movement of tools and materials and workers to the right locations, the steps necessary to perform the job, the time and money allocations involved, and the quality standards necessary. You will need to train workers to follow the systems which you set up.

On the other hand, if you are in unit or small-batch production, you will want to find the best possible people to do the jobs and will concentrate on defining the outcome expected. Unit or small-batch production requires workers with greater skill than large-batch or mass production; these workers will bring their skills to the job when you employ them. That's why Woodward found a ratio of one staff specialist per eight production workers in small-batch firms and one staff specialist per five-and-a-half production workers in large-batch firms. The latter type requires more people to plan work, schedule work, and inspect the outcome. Said another way, in large-batch operations as many standards are set ahead of time as possible, and the people setting standards and controlling the results are the staff personnel.

These relationships were indicated in a study of 79 manufacturing firms[10] which considered the relationship between the technology of the firms, degree of vertical integration involved, size, extent of decentralization, and use of sophisticated controls. In addition, the study contrasted the patterns of organization in high-profit and low-profit firms.

The results showed that the more the technology of the firm was characterized by high volume and mass production and the larger the firm's size, the more it was vertically integrated. Further, the more vertically integrated, the greater was decentralization of decision making. Finally, the more decentralized, the more the firm used sophisticated controls for quality, costing, inventory, scheduling, finances, and evaluation of executive performance. Equally important, the more profitable firms tended to follow this pattern more than less profitable firms.

In addition, as we would expect, the more standardized the technology, the more the firms were organized functionally instead of using some goal-oriented structure such as product, territory, or customer.

Considered from the standpoint of more "made-to-order" or customized technology, or from smaller firm size, this information suggests that such firms should not integrate vertically and should contain more centralized control by top management. Customized-product firms would not expect to have sophisticated controls like mass-production firms.

Now, a word of caution. People have a tendency to confuse standards of *style* with standards of *accomplishment*. Style standards include things like personal appearance, sex, education, sociability, and the like. Unless it can be demonstrated that these characteristics are directly related to successful job accomplishment, I'd forget them and concentrate on standards related to job performance.

The importance of this may be illustrated with a couple of examples. You may recall the book and Broadway show entitled *How to Succeed in Business Without Really Trying*.[11] In it an employee was advised about how to impress the boss. He was told to come in to the office early without shaving, muss his hair, pull the shades, and turn on the lights. Then the boss would come in and say, "Good Lord, are you still here?" The employee should look up and ask if it's morning already. Style versus accomplishment.

Another example involves the president of a major business machines company. He would call the plant on Saturday morning with the idea that managers who put in the extra time must be superior personnel. As a result, the Saturday Morning Club developed in the company. Managers would come in, sit around, and wait for the president to call. If he did, he noted the name of the person answering, and that person was likely to be identified as a good executive.

Instead of rewarding people for their style, I'd suggest identifying good job performance and rewarding the people who deliver the goods. You will profit and so will they.

Other Steps for Organizing Information Processing

After the policies, structure, and job standards have been set, there are still several other steps to be taken. If the organization is small or if the operations are routine and predictable, these first three steps (policies, structure, and job standards) may be enough to handle most of the information processing requirements. On the other hand, as Galbraith points out, if the operations are uncertain, with lots of exceptions, some further steps should be considered.

Reduce the need for information processing or increase the capacity for information processing. One possibility is to reduce the *need* for information processing. This may be done by either creating slack resources or by establishing self-contained organization units. Another possibility is to increase the *capacity* for information processing. This can be done either by establishing vertical information systems or by increasing the lateral relations within the structure. Let's take each of these in turn.

Reduce the need for information processing by creating slack resources. Slack resources are extra time, personnel, inventory, and the like which reduce the pressures for interdependence between parts of the organization. For example, when NASA was well funded in the late '50s and early '60s, personnel were assigned on a full-time basis to projects, and schedules were extremely tight. No one worried much about money requirements in those days; instead, all were concerned with placing a man on the moon or placing a satellite in orbit by a scheduled date. In that case slack resources were the personnel assigned to project groups on a full-time basis to reduce the problems of processing information between technical departments. As NASA's budget was cut back, a different form of slack was created. Schedules were slipped for remaining projects, and work was done in functional departments. That slack permitted work to be accomplished slowly without a lot of pressure for delivery.

In much the same way, organizations may create excess in process inventories, may develop backlogs and long delivery dates, and may reduce expected standards of performance to hold down the pressures between departments and consequent processing of information between them.

Reduce the need for information processing by creating self-contained units or organizations. As we discussed earlier, a change from a functional structure to a mixed-skill, goal-oriented structure greatly reduces the pressure for information processing between units. In functional structures the departments depend upon each other and exceptional problems can severely strain the relations between departments. On the other hand, if the organization is broken down into independent, goal-oriented units, then each unit is self-contained and need not be involved with others. Resources will be duplicated to be sure, but in goal-oriented units the survival needs of the organization are more project success and creativity than economy.

In the same way, when a large organization is subdivided into independent profit centers, the information processing required is reduced. The divisions of General Motors operate as separate companies within the corporate umbrella.

Increase the capacity for information processing by establishing vertical informational systems. The use of computerized management informational systems may be seen in the airline reservation systems, the hotel registration systems, and the control of fast food chain operations. By processing and simplifying information automatically, information processing requirements are enhanced, and exceptions may be handled more easily. Galbraith suggests that the advantage of computer processing over manual processing of quantitative information is approximately 100,000 to 1.

Information systems need not be computerized by any means. The use of a scheduling department or the use of production reports are also examples of vertical information systems.

Increase the capacity for information processing by increasing lateral contacts in the organization. I have observed a tendency in smaller organizations to take problems to the top, with relatively little cross-contact or problem solving at lower levels of the organization. For example, the president of one company that I know of had five department heads reporting to him, and he was expected to make decisions whenever an exception occurred. As the company grew, more and more pressure for decision making was placed on the president. In addition, the president developed outside interests and could spend only half of his working hours in the company. To deal with this situation, we suggested that the president encourage the department managers to make decisions as a group, rather than referring them to the president; the president readily agreed. The department managers were then trained in skills of joint decision making and proceeded to operate as a group without channeling decisions to the top.

Similar information processing capacity may be added through encouraging cross-contacts between people, through the addition of liaison people, and through the use of committees and other groups. If you haven't been using coordinating and decision-making groups, I'd suggest that you try them. You may be surprised at the quality of effort that your people turn out.

Summary

To summarize what we've said about organization design, if you want to increase the efficiency and effectiveness of your organization, you can:

- Establish rules, policies, and procedures where behavior can be anticipated.

- Publicize the present organization structure.

- Design and implement a new structure in keeping with requirements of size and technology.

- Set performance standards for activities and projects.

- Set standards on the basis of performance, not style.

- Reduce information processing requirements by creating slack resources (if appropriate).

- Reduce information processing requirements by creating self-contained units (if appropriate).

- Increase capacity for information processing by vertical information systems (if appropriate).

- Increase capacity for information processing by increasing lateral contacts in the organization (if appropriate).

Chapter 14   Job Design

The British created a civil service job in 1803 calling for a man to stand on the Cliffs of Dover with a spyglass. He was supposed to ring a bell if he saw Napoleon coming. The job was abolished in 1945.

George Sobel

Two Job Types
If we look at jobs that people perform, it is apparent that they differ widely in the amount of freedom and discretion intended. In some jobs a person will work with relatively little supervision, will make judgments about how to do the work, and will complete a whole task. Other jobs require that a person follow a specified procedure, take directions and control from a variety of sources, and perform tasks for which the purpose is fairly remote. When the job satisfaction of people doing these two general types of work is measured, it is not unusual for people with the first job arrangement to have higher satisfaction than people doing the second kind of work.

With that kind of evidence in mind, both practitioners and academicians often concluded that the way to increase satisfaction was to "enlarge" jobs, giving employees more freedom, more influence over work processes, and less direct supervision. When this change occurred, sometimes satisfaction did increase. Other times it stayed the same or actually decreased. In addition, productivity didn't always move in the same direction as satisfaction. In some cases, when satisfaction went up with job enlargement, productivity went down. Not until recently have we been able to explain why these strange things happened and to know what works when. It is now possible to suggest the proper way to design jobs so that people will be able to experience both high performance and acceptable levels of job satisfaction.

A Look at History and Research
To get an understanding of what works when, let's start with some brief history. Until the early 1940s the main preoccupation of those concerned with job design was upon how to divide the labor to make work more efficient. Where work could be divided into small repetitive tasks—whether in an office, a meat-packing company, or an automobile-assembly plant—a number of good things happened. For one thing, workers were easy to train and to replace. For another, as long as the actions of workers could be balanced, specialization increased productivity. In addition, the use of special-

ized, repetitive jobs permitted the use of specialized machines to aid in the simple jobs. This kind of work required production of a high volume of standardized goods or services, but under those circumstances, it generated efficiency and productivity.

Most of this development in our economy took place during the first forty or fifty years of this century. We don't have much information about job satisfaction during those years, but I doubt that it was particularly bad. The organization of industrial unions in the 1930s might be a sign that people weren't happy, but it seems more likely that the union movement developed to provide job security, a systematic way to solve disputes, and improved pay and benefits rather than to oppose job design itself.

Early Experience with Redesign and Enlargement
The first consideration of job redesign and enlargement started in the Endicott plant of International Business Machines in 1944. This concern appears to have been motivated more by cost and production considerations than it was by a desire to improve satisfaction. According to the story of the IBM experience, an executive was walking through the plant and noticed a worker sitting at his idle machine. When the worker was asked why he wasn't busy, he replied that he was waiting for the setup man. The executive asked: "Can't you set up the machine?" The worker replied, "Sure, but that's the job of the setup man."

Reportedly, as a result of this incident the entire production process was redesigned. Four jobs were combined: machine operator, setup man, sharpener, and inspector. One entire level of supervision was eliminated. As a result, the production costs were lowered, quality was increased, and worker morale improved. This experience at IBM seems to have triggered continuing interest in job enlargement among large numbers of organizations, including the Maytag Company, American Telephone and Telegraph, Detroit Edison, Colonial Insurance Company, the Social Security Administration, and the U.S. Civil Service. Sometimes production quality and work satisfaction increased. Sometimes volume increased, and costs were reduced. In other cases, things got worse instead of better. The differences between successful and unsuccessful forms of job design are important to us here because they help to explain what works when.

Before I get into those details, I want to mention the issue of organization size. The examples that I've given so far have concerned large organizations. Smaller enterprises are less likely to have the high degree of specialization found in larger companies, though this does not always follow. My point is that even though my examples and research reports are drawn from large companies, the lessons of job design and employee selection apply equally well to small companies.

Values Brought to the Job

The first big breakthrough in understanding the issue of job design came with the work of Charles Hulin and Milton Blood.[1] In attempting to explain their own research findings and those of others, these men found that employees seemed to bring a set of work values to the job which affected how they reacted to job enlargement. Let me back up now and explain why this fact is so important.

Hulin and Blood described the traditional way that people had been looking at job design. First, they observed that large numbers of workers were on jobs which required little skill, which repeated a short work cycle over and over, and which were closely controlled by the work system imposed. Then, they reported that to the workers these tasks seemed unimportant and monotonous, resulting in boredom and dissatisfaction with the job. They found that as a result, workers often displayed high rates of absenteeism, turnover, and restriction of output. Viewed in this way, the situation implies that the way to improve the whole mess would be to redesign the jobs so they had high skill requirements, a variety of tasks, and less control by a work system. Where this redesign did occur, the results varied. Sometimes absenteeism, turnover, and production improved; sometimes they didn't.

Hulin and Blood observed that some of the assumptions reported weren't always correct. Some workers, it seems, didn't mind routine tasks. Others reacted negatively to opportunities to make their own decisions and to think creatively about their work. Still others actually became dissatisfied when their jobs were enlarged.

In considering this puzzle, Hulin and Blood observed that previous writers seemed to assume that where workers didn't want to take responsibility in their jobs, the cause lay in the employing organizations. Such writers suggested that workers had been made dependent and unthinking by their employers. Poor attitudes about work were supposedly caused by the employers.

Those who made employers the heavy had based their case on studies of worker attitudes. For example, one study[2] which compared unskilled with skilled workers found that unskilled workers had: (1) less interest in doing high quality work; (2) less interest in learning more about their jobs; (3) more interest in money as a reward; (4) lower estimates of their own ability; (5) less desire for variety and independence in their work; (6) higher work spoilage; (7) fewer job-related friendships; and (8) less creative use of their own leisure.

Other studies reported similar findings. When the writers evaluated the situation, they did a strange thing: They *judged* these attitudes as bad or unhealthy, they *blamed* the employer for such unhealthy attitudes, and they concluded that the solution was to enlarge the jobs. Hulin and Blood observed that *maybe* these attitudes were not caused by the employer at all. Maybe the workers had the attitudes when they took their jobs. They also observed that the attitudes were merely facts and that labeling them as bad or unhealthy was unfair or mistaken. The people using those labels, they said, were merely imposing their own values on the attitudes of others.

The key to unlocking the question of why some workers actually liked more responsibility while others rejected attempts to enlarge their jobs came with the discovery that the attitudes of employees seemed to vary *depending upon where the workers lived.*

When Hulin and Blood went back and reviewed the studies on job enlargement, they found that blue-collar workers in small towns seemed to respond positively to job enlargement or to jobs in which they felt they had a great deal of responsibility. The researchers also found that blue-collar workers in large industrialized cities would often not respond positively to job enlargement and to opportunities for more responsibility. White-collar workers, on the other hand, seemed to welcome job enlargement in small or large cities.

Hulin and Blood suggested that perhaps the reason for these differences was not the effect of the job at all, but instead came from the values or attitudes that people had in the first place. People from smaller or rural backgrounds might have a set of beliefs which say that it is good to work hard, to be loyal to the employer, to advance in the job, and to take personal responsibility. In contrast, they suggested that people who had grown up in a blue-collar environment in a large city might well believe that their jobs are places to earn money for other outside satisfaction, that it is pointless to be loyal to the employer, and that attempts to advance in the job would merely be frustrating and unsuccessful.

Where workers brought the first set of beliefs to the job, they would be dissatisfied with routine work and would become more satisfied and productive with job enlargement. Where workers brought the second set of beliefs to the job, it seemed likely that they might accept the routineness of their jobs and would react negatively to job enlargement.

As further research has progressed on this subject these conclusions seem to be pointing in the right direction: attitudes brought to the job. It is not the rural or urban background which is the best predictor. Instead, it is the values of the workers which are important. Workers who prefer responsibility and enlarged jobs believe that hard work, job skill, advancement, and employer loyalty are good. Workers who do not respond do not believe in these values. In addition, workers who respond favorably to high levels of responsibility also want to gain a sense of achievement, recognition, or self-fulfillment from their jobs (called "higher-order needs"). In contrast, the other group is more concerned with pay, security, and outside sources of satisfaction (called "lower-order needs").* Neither set of values should be considered bad; the two are merely different. The important thing for us as we consider job design is to place people with a particular set of attitudes in jobs designed to meet their needs.

For example, if you employ people who do believe in the virtues of hard work and advancement, then you should put them in jobs which meet their needs or else redesign jobs to meet those needs. Similarly, if you employ people who are interested in the job only as a place to earn an income, then you should design the jobs to meet those needs. Either one is OK as long as the worker and the job design match. Later in this chapter I want to identify how to design jobs along these lines.

Characteristics of the Job

Scope and Depth
When we consider job design, it is useful to think of the job as having two dimensions which I'd like to call job depth and job scope. *Job scope* involves the variety of tasks performed. The scope of the job can be increased by adding tasks to the job or by instituting job rotation. At low skill levels this simply adds more low-skilled tasks. While rotation may help

---

*One measure of such values is a questionnaire which determines one's beliefs about the Protestant Work Ethic or Non-Protestant Work Ethic.[3] Incidentally, this has absolutely nothing to do with the Protestant religion. People high in this work ethic will strongly agree with such statements as, "Hard work makes a better person," or "A good indication of a man's worth is how well he does his job."

Another questionnaire[4] measures the preference for higher-order needs (e.g., recognition, achievement, self-realization) or for lower-order needs (e.g., pay, security). People with higher-order needs will, for example, choose a job in which they can be creative and innovative over one offering very good pay. Similarly, they will choose a job in which greater responsibility is given according to the quality of work over a job in which greater responsibility is given on the basis of seniority.

to relieve boredom, it may not meet the needs of a worker who wants challenge and significance in her job.

Job depth, on the other hand, concerns the degree of responsibility involved, or the degree to which a person is free to do things his own way. The depth in a job can be increased by giving a person a whole, natural work unit, by removing job controls, by assigning tasks which require more skill, or by making the individual personally accountable for his actions. This process is generally described as job enrichment. As I have already suggested, people with values that favor hard work and higher-order needs will generally respond favorably to increasing the depth of the job. In contrast, people who do not have such values may well respond to increases in job depth with little or no increase in satisfaction.

Current evidence seems to support the relationships just described. Recent research by Richard Hackman and Greg Oldham[5] identifies five "core dimensions" in a job which give it depth and meaningfulness if perceived by a worker as such: (1) skill variety, or the degree to which a job requires different activities and talents; (2) task identity, or the degree to which the job requires the completion of a whole and identifiable piece of work; (3) task significance, or the degree to which the job has impact on the lives or work of other people; (4) autonomy, or the degree to which the job provides freedom, independence, and personal judgment in carrying out the work, and (5) feedback, or the degree to which people doing the work have clear and direct information about the effectiveness of their individual performance.

To the extent that these five core dimensions are perceived in a job, it appears that motivation, higher performance and job satisfaction, and reduced absenteeism or turnover will occur, particularly among those workers who believe in higher-order needs for hard work, achievement, company loyalty, and the like.

Matching of Jobs and People
Where people have the ability to do enriched jobs and the values consistent with such responsibility, I'd suggest trying

to place them in jobs with a high degree of depth. Frederick Herzberg has provided a nice example of how clerical jobs were given more depth. [6] First, a list was made of changes which might enrich the jobs without concern for their practicality. Then, the list was screened to eliminate hygiene factors (i.e., such things as working conditions, supervision, or company policy), to eliminate changes in breadth rather than depth, and to eliminate generalities (e.g., give more responsibility).

As a result, clerical personnel, rather than the supervisor, signed their own correspondence, did their own proofreading, composed letters according to their own judgment, and were held individually responsible for communication with the respondent. In a training film on the same subject, Herzberg has shown how the job of salespeople was also enriched.[7] Prior to the change they had completed lengthy reports about each call, had no authority to handle complaints, could make no dollar adjustments where shipments were incorrect, and worked under the close supervision of a sales manager.

To alter the situation, a group of managers listed changes which could be made, eliminated generalities, eliminated changes which would merely increase scope like "rotate territories," and selected suggestions which would really enhance job depth. Salespeople were allowed to use their own judgment about what information should be reported to the home office. They were given the responsibility for following up on orders, making adjustments as needed. They began handling their own complaints. They were given the responsibility for the whole task of servicing their own customers. Herzberg has shown that where these changes are made, the changed group will often outperform similar groups in which the changes are not made. He reports that the only difficulty is with supervisors who are afraid that changes will result in poor performance or are uncomfortable about employees taking over responsibility that was formerly theirs.

In contrast with this process I've also seen employers move in the opposite direction. One case involved a company which required efficient mass production of a product. The company hired people who did not have higher-order needs and who saw their jobs as means to earn a living. The employer recognized the reality of his situation and took great pains to structure the job and its rewards. He carefully defined the steps in the production process. He trained people to demonstrate that they could perform at high levels if they wanted to. He made clear the rewards which would result from high performance and that they would not result from less than high performance. He recognized that such people were interested primarily in security and money. He paid people well and provided good security for the people who performed the carefully defined good job and did not reward people who did a poor job. By matching the right people with the right job design, he too had a productive, satisfied work group.

If you consider the two methods for matching people and jobs which we have been describing, you will see that there is little to be gained by criticizing people for having different kinds of attitudes toward work. Instead, you might do better to deal with the realities of your situation and either change jobs to meet the needs of your employees or get the kind of employees who will work best in the jobs you have available. Where the jobs have depth, you will want to take care to define a good job in terms of the outcome expected. That is, describe what the project, report, or product will be like if the job is done successfully. On the other hand, where the jobs are low in depth, you will want to take great pains to lay out the steps of the process required. In either case you will want to reward only good performance with rewards which employees value. People doing enriched jobs—that is, jobs with a lot of depth—will get some personal satisfaction just by doing the work and accomplishing their jobs successfully. They will also expect to be treated fairly with pay and working conditions; getting recognition, advancement, and opportunities for more growth will very likely be quite important. In contrast, people properly assigned to jobs with low depth will probably place a greater emphasis on pay, job security, and proper supervision.

This discussion about matching the right people with the right jobs suggests a number of alternatives for you.

You may want to change job designs to meet the needs of your type of employees. Where you employ people with higher needs (e.g., responsibility, advancement, hard work), you will provide a high degree of job depth; where you employ people with lower-level needs (e.g., pay, security), you may want to provide jobs with lower depth.

You may want to change the people working in your type of jobs. You will select people with needs which match the kind of job involved. In addition, you will transfer people to jobs which match their needs.

You may want to change the attitudes toward work so that people value opportunities for personal development, challenge, and freedom. Here I'd be cautious because, regardless of how worthwhile this alternative seems, it is difficult to change attitudes.

You may want to move your business to a location where the labor supply matches your kind of job design. There is still some reason to believe that blue-collar workers in rural communities will value higher-order needs more than those in large industrial centers and will respond better to enriched jobs.

Summary

To summarize what we've said about job design, if you want employees who are likely to be productive and satisfied with their work, you should:

• Provide jobs with skill variety, task identity, task significance, autonomy, and feedback to employees who value hard work, advancement, responsibility, achievement, and personal growth.

• Provide jobs with carefully detailed procedures, good pay, security, and effective supervision to employees who see the job as a place to earn a living but do not want challenge or responsibility.

• Reward people with things which they value when they

do a good job and not reward such people when they do not perform well.

• Carefully define a good job, with emphasis on outcomes or completion for people with high-depth jobs and emphasis on proper procedures for people with low-depth jobs.

Chapter 15 Selecting Good People

The best executive is the one who has enough sense to pick good men to do what he wants done, and self-restraint enough to keep from meddling with them while they do it.

Theodore Roosevelt

Value of Systematic Selection

Several years ago I had a client whose business made a piece of industrial equipment. He was a craftsman who had built his business to a sales level of about three million dollars a year. The company had its ups and downs, and the president was not particularly happy with the way it was operating. He also had reached a point in life where he wanted to do other things instead of running the organization. A colleague and I worked with the president and his managers to bring the company into the administrative type of operation. It was reorganized. The top management group learned to work together as a team. Budgeting and cost controls were installed. Production information and control systems were developed. A professional purchasing agent was employed. A management by objectives system was developed to the satisfaction of company managers. The last step was to employ a new president.

In preparing for the day when a new chief executive would take over, he and I reviewed the steps necessary for effective selection. When I didn't hear from the president for several months, I called him to find out how things were progressing. He said, "Things are fine. I just hired my replacement." When I asked him who the candidates had been, he said, "Well, Alan, we used a modified version of what you suggested." That kind of statement generally means that the person didn't do what I had recommended. It was true in this case.

I learned that the president had been anxious to have the job filled and had called a man who managed a small screw machine shop for the company and asked whether he would like to be the new president. Naturally, the man said yes. In the years which followed the new president apparently didn't succeed. Sales dropped. The company lost money. Some of the better managers quit. Finally, the new president was fired and the owner and original president is back on the job trying to rebuild the company.

I cannot prove that the new president caused the failure. From all appearances, though, he did. This case seems to illustrate that a company can pay a high price for not doing the work necessary for systematic selection. Poor selection practices are expensive. When people fail to do their jobs, they damage the company and they are expensive to replace.

Failure to perform on a job can occur from two general sources—poor ability or poor motivation. We have already discussed the basic factors involved in motivation. In this chapter I want to discuss ability—the other element involved in good performance. Ability depends upon a person's physical or mental capacity to do a job and upon the knowledge and skills gained through experience and formal learning. Obviously, a person with lots of ability and no motivation isn't going to perform well. Equally as obvious is the fact that a person with lots of motivation but no ability can't perform well.

Motivation shown on a job depends a lot on the test of time. We do the best we can to establish good motivation and then must wait to see what actually happens. When it comes to ability, though, we can tell within limits whether or not it exists before a person is employed. Thus, there is no excuse for employing people who lack the ability to do a job.

In this chapter I will be discussing some simple procedures that can be followed to increase the accuracy of employing able people. Before discussing those procedures, though, let me discuss a closely related problem.

Hiring from Outside or Promoting from Within
An alternative to selection from outside the company is promoting from within. Internal promotion definitely has advantages, and the policy is appealing to people within the company who want to climb the ladder. If people can be trained systematically, there can be great assurance that they will have the necessary ability to do the job. Training is easiest where the company has an effective training program and where there are relatively large numbers of people doing similar work. Where there are large numbers of similar employees, the company with a good training program can employ relatively inexpensive, untrained people and move them to more demanding jobs as their skills are increased. This is most likely in functional organizations discussed in Chapter

12. Let's consider a different situation.

Suppose Good Old Joe is working in the plating department. He has worked for the company for twelve years, and it is difficult to keep giving him raises since he is already making more money than the other workers. Top management gets together and says, "What are we going to do about Good Old Joe?"

"What do you mean?"

"We can't keep giving him raises every year without doing something else."

"Then why don't we make him a foreman of the plating department?"

"Do you think he can do it?"

"I don't know, but we can't afford to lose his talents. He knows things about the plating process that no one else seems to know."

So Good Old Joe is made the foreman. When the manager asks Joe's subordinates about obstacles to their performance and satisfaction, it is not uncommon for them to complain that Joe won't tell them how to do the job. They say, "That's easy. I want to learn this job and advance in the company, and I have tried to get Joe to train me. Just recently I said, 'Joe, would you explain to me how that plating machine operates.' Joe said, 'I told you once, Dummy, do I have to tell you again?' Well, that hurt my feelings. I've stopped asking."

Part of the difficulty with Joe may be his inability to train others. Part, though, is likely to be his understanding of his own power. Joe says to himself, "They promoted me because they can't afford to lose me. I know stuff that no one else knows." Joe has power and influence because of his special knowledge. Conclusion: If he trains others so that they know what he knows, he won't have his power anymore. So Joe does the sensible thing: He keeps his skills a secret.

But you as a manager may have hired a foreman from outside the company and found he didn't work out. The stories I have heard about bringing in outside people relate to what I have come to call the SOB principle. It may be stated as follows: Without systematic selection, employing people from outside can make internal people who were ignored very testy. For example, suppose that B is the executive and that S reports to B. One day B announces that he has employed Mr. O from outside the company and that from then on S will report to O and O will report to B. At this point it is not uncommon for S to say, "That SOB! I helped him make this company a success. I worked long hours on my own in the old plant. I told B how to run his company. Now, when the company is a success, they bring in this ding-a-ling from outside and pay him a big salary. O didn't pay his dues around here. Phooey."

Basic Rules for Selection

Fortunately, there are some simple rules which will minimize the problem of the Good Old Joes and the SOB principle. They involve a systematic selection process to make sure that people have ability as well as a mechanism to learn what is required in a job.

Now let's turn to the selection process and see how this can work. I will be discussing three main rules: (1) select to standard, (2) use valid selection methods, and (3) use an appropriate selection ratio.

1. *Select to standard.* By selecting to standard I mean that any selection which is going to be effective will start with a specific statement of the abilities, responsibilities, and performance requirements of the job. The standard is expressed in a job description which either indicates the work requirements in the job or which indicates the difference between good and bad performance in a job. For example, a job description of that first type will generally include supervision given and received; a list of the different kinds of duties performed; responsibilities for people or equipment; job knowledge necessary; mental and physical demands; and relationship to other jobs for advancement. This presents a word picture of the job without indicating good or bad behavior itself.

Another approach does provide an indication of effective or ineffective job behavior. It is developed by determining the behavior exhibited by effective performers that is not exhibited by poor performers. For example, a sales job may be described effectively as calling on customers immediately upon receipt of customer complaint, discussing complaints with customers, planning each day's activities before starting work, calling on all accounts systematically, being truthful with customers, checking with customers after delivery, and so on. This kind of description is particularly useful in evaluating work performance and in coaching to improve performance.

Information about job standards is generally obtained from people in the job or from those who are well acquainted with it. Even though consultants or staff specialists can be helpful in determining the process for obtaining information or the form in which to express it, the job content information is best derived from those in or near the job.

Job dimensions described should cover all key areas of job performance. They should be broken down into categories of performance and, if appropriate, the relative importance to job success of various categories should be specified.

2. *Use valid selection methods.* Valid selection methods are those which predict accurately; reliability contributes importantly to validity. Reliability means that the same measure will be obtained if the method is repeated. One particularly useful principle for selection is the fact that *the best predictor of future behavior is past behavior in a similar situation.* That is, past behavior is often a valid and reliable indicator of performance ability in the future under similar conditions.

This principle is useful where an organization has difficulty in training people for a job and where it wishes to guarantee performance potential. Think about it. Even if you have the ability to construct your own car, it is far easier to go to an automobile dealer and buy a car which has already been tested. The best predictor of future behavior is past behavior. Similarly, if you are the coach of the Green Bay Packers, it is far easier to scout and hire good college players than it is to find young men and teach them to play football.

The best predictor of future behavior is past behavior.

I emphasize this point because I have seen small companies try over and over to make specialists out of generalists from within the company. A foreman is made head of a new production control department. An employee with a bad back which prevents him from lifting heavy objects is made personnel manager. An old salesman who can't travel anymore is made purchasing agent. Often these employees fail. If they do continue in the job, it may be because there is no way to know whether or not they are doing a good job with no one to compare them to. It may be better to employ a person who has already demonstrated high performance skills. Note that I am not saying that such people can't be good specialists. I am only suggesting that it may be more effective to find someone who has already demonstrated motivation and ability in the job than to train someone to do it.

The actual process for establishing validity of selection methods is fairly straightforward. One method is to employ people using the present methods of selection but to obtain information at the same time from tests, structured interviews, and application blanks. Then, after the people employed have learned their jobs and exhibited their expected level of job competence, the original information is correlated with their level of performance. For example, suppose a company hires salespeople with its old method and obtains test information as well. Later, when they have learned their jobs, their performances are measured. If those with the lowest scores on the test have the poorest performances, those with the next higher scores have the next highest performances, and so on up to top performers, then there is a positive correlation between the test score and the job performance. The test predicts subsequent job performance. The statistics used to express this relationship will show the degree to which the test predicts actual performance from zero, when there is absolutely no relationship, to plus or minus one, when there is a perfect relationship.

Certainly organizations ought to validate their selection information. The fact is, however, most can't or don't. They can't when there aren't enough people employed in similar jobs to make such analysis possible. They don't because they lack the motivation or ability to do so.

If you can validate your selection methods, by all means do it. If you can't, then I'd like to suggest some things which you can do to improve the validity and reliability of your selection methods. One, of course, is to employ people who have already demonstrated the performance which you want. Even if the new job is not exactly like the old one, there may be similarities in some parts of the two jobs. A careful statement of the job standards will often indicate similar categories in which past behaviors can be compared with those in a future job. For example, if the candidate had a supervisory job and your open position calls for similar supervisory responsibility, you can find out the extent to which the candidate structured the work to be done, exhibited consideration of subordinate needs, trained subordinates, was clear and consistent in giving directions, put policies in writing, and so on.

Another thing you can do is to improve your interviewing methods. Most personnel books will tell you that interviews are terrible measures of ability. Indeed they are, but they are also the most popular selection tool. It seems sensible to try to make this popular tool somewhat better than it usually is. With this in mind, I'd suggest the following.

Gather interview information about the job requirements stated in the job description. Even though several interviewers will agree on the facts, they will often disagree about the degree of candidate quality. Apparently people compare candidates with their own stereotypes of quality; this tendency may be reduced by focusing on the requirements stated in the job description.

Consider all relevant information. Without care, unfavorable information tends to be weighted more heavily by interviewers than favorable information. Because of this, a good candidate with strong credentials but with a negative factor may be weighted less favorably than a mediocre candidate with no negative factors. All information should be considered.

Ask all candidates the same questions in the same way. By using a structured interview schedule with standard questions, you will obtain information that will be more comparable among candidates.

Record interview responses for later consideration. Some effective interviewers will take notes during the interview. Others will tape the responses for later transcription. The purpose of the interview is to gather information for consideration later, *not* to make judgments about candidates at the time.

Compare information about all the candidates at the same time. Interviewers who make judgments in an interview often draw their conclusion within the first five minutes of the session. By withholding judgment until all candidates are considered in each of the job performance categories, you probably can make more factual and more valid judgments.

Increase reliability by using multiple measures of the same thing. Several questions asked about the same thing will be more reliable than a single question. Similarly, several raters will provide more reliable judgments than a single rater. One can improve the reliability and validity of judgments by having several qualified people consider the facts independently for each of the candidates in each of the job performance categories and then bringing these judges together to discuss and agree on their conclusions.

If you use tests for selection, they should be validated. There are basically four classes of tests available. The first class includes aptitude tests. They measure intellectual ability in a variety of areas such as numerical calculation, verbal comprehension, or abstract reasoning. For some occupations, different aptitudes have been shown to be highly related to job success. The second class of instruments includes so-called achievement tests. In general, aptitude tests attempt to assess what a person *can learn,* while achievement tests assess what a person *has learned.* Such tests are designed to measure knowledge associated with a trade or the ability to perform some kind of work—typing skill, for example.

The third class of tests includes measures of personality. For example, one measure determines the extent to which people have preferences for situations which provide them with a strong sense of achievement or the ability to work closely with people or the opportunity to dominate and control others. The fourth category of tests includes preferences for vocational activities. For example, such a test may assess the extent to which a person favors activities which are computational, scientific, or persuasive. Different occupations have been shown to relate to different patterns of such choices.

My purpose in this brief reference to testing is twofold. For one thing, it is to alert you to the fact that tests should not be lumped into one category. To be "for" or "against" tests makes about as much sense as being for or against animals. There are many different types.

The other reason for mentioning tests is to emphasize that they can be a useful tool if they are validated in your own organization. Under the Civil Rights Act of 1964, it is necessary to show that tests used for selection or other purposes are valid predictors of successful job behavior and that they do not discriminate with respect to minority groups. The law does permit the use of tests which have been validated in jobs similar to those in your organization. Your federal or state employment service can give you information about those which would be acceptable in your company. Again, however, validity cannot be assured unless it is established in your own organization.

3. *Use an appropriate selection ratio.* The selection ratio is the number of qualified people considered to fill a job. Even if you can't do a great deal to increase the validity of your selection methods, you can increase your selection effectiveness simply by increasing the number of qualified people that you consider for a job. This is important. It is something that most employers can do rather easily.

Basically, the reasoning is this: If you have a 100 percent valid selection device, you can employ the first person who meets your standards. You can employ the first person who applies if that person qualifies for the job. On the other hand, *as the validity of your selection process goes down, you can compensate by increasing the number of people considered for the job.* Said another way, if you have any validity to your present selection methods, by increasing the number of qualified people considered for a job, you can *automatically* increase the average quality of your work force. There is absolutely no magic, theory, or opinion about this. It is a simple fact of numbers. It is something that you can start to do immediately to improve your selection process.

An Example of Selection
To show how this process can operate, let me describe an example which happened recently. A client of mine called one day to report that his plant manager had died suddenly of a heart attack. There was no one present who could train a new plant manager and a natural replacement did not exist in the company. The president was concerned, however, that bringing in an outsider for the position might antagonize present supervisors.

The first step in finding a replacement was to prepare a detailed job description for the plant manager position. The president and others familiar with the job were asked to list all of the activities performed by the plant manager. These were then grouped into key areas of responsibility including: personnel, equipment, production planning and control, physical maintenance of the plant, control of production costs, and development of employee skills. Next, an interview schedule was prepared asking questions about demonstrated ability in the various areas of responsibility.

The company then solicited resumes from people interested in the position through blind ads in four periodicals, through industry contacts, and by posting the job opening for people within the company. In all, 157 applications for the position were received. The resumes were then categorized independently by the consultant and by the president; eight candidates were finally selected.

A panel of judges was selected for final screening which included a corporate board member, a retired company president, the current president, the consultant, and an elected representative from the supervisory group. These people were present when the eight candidates were interviewed over a two day period. The president and the consultant divided the task of asking questions in the structured interview and, in addition, other questions were asked by all members of the panel of judges. Each person took notes and interviews were tape recorded as well. Panel members were cautioned to avoid making judgments at the time; they were only to obtain information.

Following the interviews, panel members evaluated each of the candidates on a numerical scale from one to ten for each job category. Then, panel ratings were posted and adjusted, if necessary, following group discussion. The process yielded two top candidates for the plant manager's job and these were further screened by the president through personal conversations and investigation of prior work history. From all appearances, the new plant manager is effective and also has the support of the supervisory group.

Application of the Rules

Applying the preceding three basic rules will help to avoid the SOB principle and the Good Old Joe problem mentioned earlier. By making jobs available to present employees as well as to outsiders, you will give people within the company a chance to advance themselves but also insure that they are able to do what is required in the new job. By having job standards clearly stated, employees learn what is necessary in the new job. If they don't have the ability to perform in the new job, they have a chance to obtain that ability.

For example, suppose Good Old Joe says, "I would like to be foreman of the plating department." Then, instead of blind promotion or rejection, you can say, "Okay, when the job opens up, I'd be glad to have you apply. Here are the job requirements. Let's review them and, if there are areas in which you seem not to be prepared, we can arrange to send you to evening courses or workshops to get the necessary skills. Or, we can develop a training program with the present foreman to bring you up to the necessary standards. This doesn't guarantee that you will get the job since we will want to consider several qualified people, but it will certainly increase your chances of getting it."

The process described will also make it easier to bring in outsiders since it educates everyone to the job requirements and since it gives all appropriate people—inside and outside the company—a chance to apply. In selecting people for key management positions, I have seen all the candidates leave the interview saying, "Wow, I didn't realize that a person had to know all of that to be chief executive of this company. I sure don't know all those things." In that case, when the best person is selected, she can be given training in areas of weakness, and the other candidates will generally give the new person their support.

Summary

To summarize, if you want to increase your chances of selecting good people, you can:

- Define job standards.

- Use valid selection methods.

- Compare expected behavior of candidates with past behavior in similar situations.

- Improve the quality of interviews.

- Use multiple measures or multiple judges to increase reliability.

- Validate and use selection tests.

- Use an appropriate selection ratio.

- Make new jobs available to people from within and outside the organization.

- Provide opportunities for present employees to improve their skills to prepare for future advancement opportunities.

Chapter 16 Finding Resources and Advice

No grand idea was ever born in a conference, but a lot of foolish ideas have died there.

F. Scott Fitzgerald, "Note-Books," *The Crack Up*

When many are got together, you can be guided by him whose counsel is wisest. . . . If a man is alone he is less full of resource, and his wit is weaker.

Homer, *The Iliad*

Anyone can hold the helm when the sea is calm.

Publilius Syrus

Amateurs versus Experts

I have gone sailing twice with a friend in the Caribbean on a bare-boat charter. Such a charter is like a rented condominium—it's a boat turned over to a company by its owner for rental by other people. The boat is provisioned and outfitted, and the renter is free to sail it on his own. My friend is a skilled sailor, and I am a novice. On one occasion we sailed the Exuma chain of islands. The side of the islands toward the mainland is shallow and sandy. About the only trouble one can get into is to get stuck on the sand and then wait for high tide to get free. The ocean side has high winds which blow toward the islands.

On the first trip we sailed north along the inland side, and I began to think, "Even I could do this. It's easy." On the return trip we used the motor to pass between two islands out into deep water. Once out, we planned to have a hard sail south. When we motored between the two islands into deep water, one of the ropes wound around the drive shaft and killed the engine. We found ourselves being blown rapidly into the rocks. My friend grabbed one of the sails and managed to maneuver us with the wind back between the islands where we dropped anchor and freed the rope.

That experience left a lasting impression on me. It is likely that we would have been seriously injured or even killed if he had not known what to do in the emergency. I was impressed by the fact that it is the experts who know what to do in the exceptional circumstances. Anyone can handle things when they are routine. Now, when I have a problem, I go ask people for information. When I do that, I'm not interested in amateurs. I get information from people who have already demonstrated that they know what they are talking about. I want information and service from professionals, not amateurs.

Sources of Part-Time Staff

Big business has the advantage of having lots of professionals on the payroll. It is not unusual for 25 to 50 percent of the people employed in a large company to be staff specialists. These are people who give service, advice, or control to the company—the lawyers, accountants, engineers, personnel managers, purchasing agents, production controllers, and the like. Most companies are too small to employ staff specialists, however. They have to get their expert information from outside the company, if they get it at all.

For those managers who do not have the luxury of company-employed staff services at their disposal, I'd like to suggest some sources of what might be called part-time staff. They are people who are available to give you professional service at minimal or no expense.

The Board of Directors
The first source I'd suggest is the board of directors. If you are the chief executive in a company which is incorporated, and if your directors' meeting consists of calling your mother (a stockholder) once a year to say, "Hi, Ma, this is our directors' meeting," then consider the alternative of a working board. There are many people whose time is ordinarily either very expensive or inaccessible who would be happy to serve on your board.

In offering some suggestions about organizing the board, I want to emphasize that these are qualified suggestions. Where present practices are known, they are offered as benchmarks. Where my own opinions are presented, they are labeled as such. In general, you should do what seems sensible to you, but you can consider the following suggestions.

Size. A survey of directorship practices published by the National Industrial Conference Board in 1973[1] indicated that the median board size for 511 manufacturers was 11; for manufacturers with assets of less than 10 million it was 6 members. In 30 retail and wholesale firms the median size was 11. In my opinion, there are rarely good reasons for having more than 7 members on the board of directors. A larger group is susceptible to more conflict and is going to have greater difficulty arriving at agreement.

Composition. There is also good reason to suggest that you have a majority of outside directors on your board. Indeed, 71 percent of the manufacturing companies in the

NICB survey had a majority of outside directors, and 86 percent of the nonmanufacturing companies surveyed had a majority of outsiders. One reason for such a practice is that you have access to the insiders any time you like. The board gives you a chance to draw on resources that you don't already have.

Small companies, in particular, need strong, independent people on their boards. The reality is that in large, publicly held companies the board hires and fires the president. In small, closely held corporations, on the other hand, the president really hires and fires the board. Thus, if the board in the small company is to be influential, the contributions of the members must be so useful that the president doesn't want to lose them.

Typical backgrounds of directors are suggested from the NICB survey, which reported that for manufacturing companies the six most frequent occupations of outside directors were manufacturing, banking, law, retirement, investments, and education. For nonmanufacturing companies they were banking, manufacturing, law, investments, retirement, and merchandising. There is no magic in this. In fact, rather than follow common practice, you can list the kinds of resources or information needed in your company and then get directors on that basis. For example, if the company is in the promotion stage and wants to become an administrative type, then I'd look for someone who has already taken a company out of the promotion period and into the administrative type. After all, the best predictor of future behavior is past behavior.

Compensation. The first thing to remember about payment of outside directors is that in most cases the payment is a token. Most directors can probably earn much more money for their time than they receive for serving on a board. In fact, compensation practices vary widely. The NICB survey found that manufacturing firms with assets of less than 10 million dollars paid a median of $100 a meeting to outside directors, while the median figure for all manufacturers was $616. The smaller figure is based on only 11 companies, but my experience with small company boards suggests that from

$100 to $250 a meeting is not unusual.

Some closely held companies pay their owner-members substantial sums for serving on the boards. The advantage here is that the payments are an expense to the corporations and are taxed only once. If the money were paid to owners as dividends, it would be taxed twice—once as corporate income and again as personal income to the owners.

Standing committees. It is common practice for boards to have standing committees. Common subcommittees include executive, salary, stock option, and audit and finance committees. These and other special committees of the board make judgments for the board or recommendations to it. The executive committee, in particular, can meet during periods when the full board does not meet.

Obtaining directors. As with any selection process, it is wise to describe the job requirements of a director in writing, use a valid selection process, and consider several candidates for the position of director. I doubt that you can actually interview prospective candidates—though the practice is not unheard of—but you can at least check out the people considered. In any case, it is important to provide the prospective director with clear expectations about what she would do on the board.

Indemnification and liability insurance. It is almost universal practice for companies to indemnify directors against losses sustained personally for legal actions arising from their activities as board members. In addition, there is increasing use of directors and officers liability insurance. This insurance is expensive, and prices for the same coverage vary widely between carriers. In all cases, you should get bids for such insurance from several carriers to compare costs and coverage.

My experience with smaller companies indicates that they often overlook the important advantages of a board of directors.

The Small Business Administration
The Small Business Administration was created by Congress in 1953. Since that time it has been an important source of

financial and managerial assistance to small businesses. There is little doubt that the SBA has been disappointing and frustrating to many. It is underfunded, bureaucratic, and often poorly staffed. Its administrators have generally been competent, dedicated people; but the delivery of services at the local level has been both good and bad. Its programs are not to be ignored, however, and I have met many business people who have been pleased by them.

If, for some reason, you seek service from the SBA, and it is not satisfactory, I'd suggest that you write to the Washington office or to the Senate Subcommittee on Small Business. The SBA generally has needed resources somewhere, but you may have to prod them into action.

Service Corps of Retired Executives (SCORE). The SCORE program is an organization of retired business executives who provide consulting which is essentially free, covering only out-of-pocket expenses. There are an estimated 4,000 volunteers throughout the country; they may be contacted through the local SBA office.

Active Corps of Executives (ACE). The ACE program is similar to SCORE but involves active executives. There are about half as many ACE volunteers as SCORE volunteers, and they are mainly in larger cities. Again, they are available through the local SBA office.

Small Business Institute (SBI). The SBA's newest management assistance program is the SBI. Through it, small businesses receive free consulting services from faculty or students at a nearby school of business. The SBA pays a small sum of money to the school for each client served. Unfortunately, participation in the SBI program is limited at present to SBA clients. I have heard many positive statements about the quality of service under the SBI program.

Your Local College
There are several ways that you can make use of your local college for part-time staff services. First, you can employ students part time for projects or in the summer. This will give you a chance to look them over for possible employment in the future, and it will give them business experience. Sec-

ond, you can make your business available for field studies by students. Some colleges require that their students do studies of businesses; these studies benefit both the company and the students. In such cases, you should require both a written and a verbal report of findings.

To illustrate the value of student efforts, I'll tell you my experience in teaching an advanced seminar in consulting methods for business students who already have the technical knowledge, but who need to learn clinical skills necessary to be a consultant. Each student in the seminar is required to consult with an organization—profit or nonprofit—up to the point that a report is made to the client about problems and their possible solutions. The process is carried out under my supervision at no cost to the client. The benefits to the clients have been substantial, and in some cases the clients have asked the students to continue the consulting relationship until the recommended actions are carried out to completion.

Another way you can make use of your local college is to get acquainted with the faculty. For example, I know one man who has what I call a "take a professor to lunch program." He will call a faculty member and say, "Hello, my name is so and so. Alan Filley says that you are the person to call if I have questions about employee selection procedures." Then, this president of a small engineering company will arrange to have lunch with the person. During lunch he will ask some questions that he would like to have answered and before lunch is over will ask for the name of a faculty member who is an expert in another subject. To my knowledge, he has had lunch with members of our department of management and with faculty in industrial engineering and computer science. In addition, he has gotten leads on good students whom he subsequently employed.

If you are worried about taking advantage of the faculty members with this process, you ought to know that it will probably be viewed quite positively rather than as an imposition. Good business schools reward their faculty these days on the basis of three criteria: research, quality teaching, and public service. *You,* the manager, are part of the public. By providing an opportunity for the faculty member to be of service to you, you are enhancing that person's opportunity for pay or promotion.

Consultants

Faculty members and others can also be employed as consultants. Used properly, consultants can be inexpensive compared with the value of their services. Since anyone can call himself a consultant, it is important to check the person's performance. Once again, the best predictor of future behavior is past behavior. I would suggest that you ask the potential consultant for a list of clients; then contact those people to find out what kind of service the consultant provided and how successful it was. As in the employment of any specialist or adviser, it is a good idea to interview several to find one you think you can or should work with.

If possible, pay the consultant for direct services rendered—either according to contracted project costs or according to hours or days provided. It is generally not a good idea to pay a consultant on a retainer. Retainers are wonderful for consultants since they are guaranteed income, but they are a disadvantage for the client since work is not tied to pay.

I'd be careful of management consultants who contact you and offer to analyze your business for little or no expense. In some cases such organizations will give you a report that will curl your hair and then offer to solve what appear to be terrible problems for a substantial sum of money. Good consultants should be able to outline their plan before they do anything and should give you a clear indication of the costs involved.

Other Executives

Top executives in small companies are pretty isolated from other professional managers. In companies with functional organizations, they are the only general executive. It is common practice for professionals like accountants or engineers who work in organizations which do not have other similar professionals to hang around with others in the profession. That is, they typically belong to local associations or attend professional meetings to find out what is going on in their specialty. Professional administrators should do the same.

One format for such association is an executive club, like that mentioned in Chapter 11. Such clubs are organized by a commercial firm which brings together groups of about nine top executives. Each group meets together once a month to hear a visiting expert on some subject. Generally, the members pay $250 a month to the company which organized the groups. The organizing company arranges for the meetings, invites the experts, and provides some degree of information and consulting to the members. Members gain information from the experts, from the company, and from other members.

You can organize such a club yourself if you want to. From my experience in helping groups to organize their own clubs, I have observed that groups often feel it is easier and more economical to have a commercial organization handle the details for the members.

Even if you don't choose to belong to one of these clubs, you will gain information just by spending time with other successful executives, either in service clubs or in one-to-one meetings.

Trade Associations

Associations of people in the same kind of business also can be useful. For example, two services provided by good associations are their cost-of-doing-business surveys and their staffing surveys. Cost-of-doing-business surveys typically show expense and profit ratios for companies, broken down by company size or type. They can be helpful in indicating whether your costs are out of line and in planning internal standards to increase profits.

Staffing surveys show the percentage of the work force employed in different kinds of jobs. They can show, for example, the point at which it is economical to employ a full-time professional purchasing agent, accountant, or personnel manager. The surveys can indicate the number of foremen or supervisors which are required at different levels of company size. They can show the typical order in which specialists are employed in the industry. Both this and the business cost survey are relatively easy to provide; if you aren't getting such information from your association, I'd suggest that you ask for it.

Trade associations also give you a chance to find out about new technology in the industry, practices of successful companies, sources of employees, and many other things.

Workshops

Adult education is big business, and it is getting bigger. Both private organizations and universities provide two- or three-day workshops and short courses for practitioners. The difference between these and regular college classes is that workshops are consumer controlled. By this I mean that they exist in a competitive market, and they have to deliver the goods or else they don't stay around. People who present workshops will typically have a depth of knowledge in their subject and platform skills which make their presentations interesting.

Workshops are typically tightly structured to give you a lot of information in a short period of time. To find out the effectiveness of workshops, you can ask their sponsors for a list of people who have attended the same workshop in the past. Call some of these people and find out what they have to say. As always, the best predictor of future behavior is past behavior in a similar situation.

Other Sources

Obviously there are many more sources of part-time staff. I have not discussed employing moonlighters or retired executives, nor have I discussed information from suppliers, customers, or even competitors. I'm sure that it is apparent, though, that there are lots of sources. You just have to look for them.

If you are a professional manager, you can benefit greatly by spending time with people who are also managers, and you can gain useful information from people who are experts in other fields. In particular, if you are the chief executive in a small company which can't employ staff specialists, then you can receive similar services by taking advantage of outsiders as part-time staff.

Epilog

This completes our discussion of management skills. If I have been successful in my effort, you should have gained information which, when applied, will increase your performance and your satisfaction as a manager.

As suggested in the foreword, this book attempts to start from the place where a manager is now and to help him make things better. There are many excellent books on this subject, but they often start with ideal practice; the leap from where the manager is to the point described by these books can be great and discouraging.

Like the new fisherman who is told to catch a fish, you can have a positive experience with skills described here, which may encourage you to gain further knowledge about the profession of management.

There has been enough food to sustain life, enough failure to enforce humility, enough love to provide comfort, . . . and except for the time I was crying it has been a very merry trip.

Arthur Berggren

Notes

Preface
1. S. R. Slaymaker II. *Simplified fly fishing.* New York: Harper and Row, 1969.
2. A. C. Filley, R. J. House, and S. Kerr. 2nd ed. *Managerial process and organizational behavior.* Glenview, Ill.: Scott, Foresman, 1976.

Chapter 1
1. J. P. Getty. *How to be a successful executive.* Chicago: Playboy Press, 1971.
2. C. I. Barnard. *The functions of the executive.* 30th anniversary ed. Cambridge, Mass.: Harvard University Press, 1968.

Chapter 2
1. A. C. Filley. The parable of the traffic light: Uses and misuses of rules. *MSU Business Topics,* Vol. 24, No. 4, 1976, pp. 57-59.

Chapter 3
1. D. C. Pelz, and F. M. Andrews. *Scientists in organizations.* New York: John Wiley & Sons, 1966.

Chapter 5
1. F. Herzberg, B. Mausner, and B. Snyderman. 2nd ed. *The motivation to work.* New York: John Wiley & Sons, 1959.
2. R. M. Stogdill, *Individual Behavior and Group Achievement.* Oxford: Oxford University Press, 1959.

Chapter 6
1. O. F. Collins, D. G. Moore, and D. B. Unwalla. *The enterprising man.* East Lansing: Michigan State University, 1964.

2. G. L. Litwin, and J. A. Ciarlo. "Achievement motivation and risk taking in a business setting." General Electric Company Behavioral Research Service, n. d.
3. O. F. Collins et al., 1964.
4. R. Bolt. "Lawrence of Arabia." A Sam Spiegel Production for Columbia Pictures, Hollywood, Calif., 1962.
5. R. M. Stogdill, and A. E. Coons, eds. *Leader behavior: Its description and measurement.* Research Monograph 88, Bureau of Business Research. Columbus, Ohio: Ohio State University, 1957.
6. R. J. House. A path goal theory of leader effectiveness. *Administrative Science Quarterly,* Vol. 16, No. 3, 1971, pp. 321-338.
7. N. V. Peale. *The power of positive thinking.* Englewood Cliffs, N.J.: Prentice-Hall, 1952.
8. D. Carnegie. *How to win friends and influence people.* New York: Simon and Schuster, 1937.

Chapter 7
1. Herzberg et al., 1959.
2. E. E. Lawler, III. *Motivation in work organizations.* Monterey, Calif.: Brooks-Cole, 1973.
3. V. H. Vroom. *Work and motivation.* New York: John Wiley & Sons, 1964.
4. E. Berne. *Happy valley.* New York: Grove Press, 1968, p. 14.
5. E. A. Locke, N. Cartledge, and C. S. Knerr. Studies of the relationship between satisfaction, goal-setting, and performance. *Organizational Behavior and Human Performance,* Vol. 5, No. 2, 1970, pp. 135-139, 151-158.
6. H. L. Tosi, and S. J. Carroll. Managerial reactions to management by objectives. *Academy of Management Journal,* Vol. 11, No. 4, 1968, pp. 415-426; and H. L. Tosi, and S. J. Carroll. Some structural factors related to goal influence in the management by objectives process. *MSU Business Topics,* Spring 1969, pp. 45-50.

Chapter 8
1. A. Delbecq, A. H. Vandeven, and D. H. Gustafson. *Group techniques for program planning.* Glenview, Ill.: Scott, Foresman, 1975.
2. N. R. F. Maier. *Problem solving and creativity in individuals and groups.* Monterey, Calif.: Brooks-Cole, 1970. See also A. C. Filley. *Interpersonal conflict resolution.* Glenview, Ill.: Scott, Foresman, 1975.
3. K. Thomas. Conflict and conflict management, in M. D. Dunnette, ed., *Handbook of industrial and organizational psychology.* Chicago: Rand McNally, 1976.
4. C. B. Derr. Managing organization conflict: A place for collaboration, bargaining and power approaches. *California Management Review,* in press.
5. A. C. Filley. *Interpersonal conflict resolution.* Glenview, Ill.: Scott, Foresman, 1975.
6. T. Harris. *I'm ok–you're ok: A practical guide to transactional analysis.* New York: Harper and Row, 1969.
7. M. James, and D. Jongeward. *Born to win: Transactional analysis with gestalt experiments.* Reading, Mass.: Addison-Wesley, 1971.

Chapter 9
1. A. Maslow. A dynamic theory of human motivation. *Psychological Review,* Vol. 50, 1943, pp. 370-373.
2. L. J. Peter, and R. Hull. *The Peter principle.* New York: William Morrow, 1969.
3. V. H. Vroom, and P. W. Yetton. *Leadership and decision making.* Pittsburgh, Pa.: University of Pittsburgh Press, 1973. See also V. H. Vroom. A new look at managerial decision making. *Organizational Dynamics,* Spring 1973, pp. 66-80.
4. N. R. F. Maier, A. Solem, and A. A. Maier. *Supervisory and executive development.* New York: John Wiley & Sons, 1957. Later published as *The role-play technique: A handbook for management and leadership practice,*

rev. ed. La Jolla, Calif.: University Associates, 1975.

Chapter 10

1. J. E. Orme. *Time, experience and behaviour.* New York: American Elsevier, 1969.

2. R. A. Mackenzie. *The time trap.* New York: AMACOM (American Management Association), 1972.

Chapter 11

1. W. Oncken, Jr., and D. L. Wass. Management, time: Who's got the monkey? *Harvard Business Review,* Vol. 52, No. 6, 1974, pp. 75-80.

2. A. Delbecq et al., 1975.

Chapter 12

1. R. Pirsig. *Zen and the art of motorcycle maintenance.* New York: William Morrow, 1974.

2. J. D. Thompson. *Organizations in action.* New York: McGraw-Hill, 1967.

3. K. D. Mackenzie. "A theory of group structure," monograph. Lawrence, Kans.: University of Kansas, 1975. See K. D. Mackenzie. *A theory of group structures.* 2 vols. New York: Gordon and Breach Science Publications, 1976.

4. A. C. Filley et al., 1976.

Chapter 13

1. J. Galbraith. *Designing complex organizations.* Reading, Mass.: Addison-Wesley, 1973. See also J. Galbraith. *Organization design.* Reading, Mass.: Addison-Wesley, 1977.

2. L. Van Beck. *The company policy manual.* Champaign, Ill.: Research Press, 1978.

3. Exodus 18: 17–36.

4. A. Child. Predicting and understanding organization structure. *Administrative Science Quarterly,* Vol. 18,

No. 2, 1973, pp. 168-185.

5. J. Woodward. *Industrial organization: Theory and practice.* London: Oxford University Press, 1965.

6. A. C. Filley, and R. Aldag. "Studies in small business organization." Madison, Wis.: University of Wisconsin, Graduate School of Business, n. d.

7. D. M. Blau, C. M. Falbe, W. McKinley, and P. K. Tracy. Technology and organization in manufacturing. *Administrative Science Quarterly,* Vol. 21, No. 1, 1976. pp. 20-40.

8. B. E. De Spalder. *Ratios of staff to line personnel.* Monograph 106, Bureau of Business Research. Columbus, Ohio: Ohio State University, 1962.

9. Graphic Arts Industries Association. *1976-1977 Canadian ratios for profit planning.* Ottawa, Canada, 1977.

10. P. N. Khandwalla. Mass output orientation of operations technology and organizational structure. *Administrative Science Quarterly,* Vol. 19, No. 1, 1974, pp. 74-97.

11. F. Loesser, music and lyrics. "How to succeed in business without really trying," 1962. Based on the script by A. Burrows, J. Weinstock, W. Gilbert, and F. Loesser. Beressord Productions Limited and Frank Loesser, 1962. Based on the book by Shepherd Mead. *How to succeed in business without really trying.* New York: Simon and Schuster, 1962.

Chapter 14

1. C. L. Hulin, and M. R. Blood. Job enlargement, individual differences and worker responses. *Psychological Bulletin,* Vol. 69, No. 1, 1968, pp. 41-55.

2. C. Argyris. The individual and organization: An empirical test. *Administrative Science Quarterly,* Vol. 4, No. 2, 1959, pp. 145-167.

3. M. R. Blood. Work values and job satisfaction. *Journal of Applied Psychology,* Vol. 53, No. 6, 1969, pp. 456-459.

4. J. R. Hackman, and E. E. Lawler, III. Employee reactions to job characteristics. *Journal of Applied Psychology*. Monograph 55, 1971, pp. 250-286.

5. J. R. Hackman, and G. R. Oldham. The job diagnostics survey: An instrument for the diagnosis of jobs in the evaluation of job redesign projects. New Haven, Conn.: Yale University, Technical Report No. 4, Department of Administrative Sciences, May 1974.

6. F. Herzberg. One more time: How do you motivate employees? *Harvard Business Review,* Vol. 46, No. 1, 1968, pp. 53-62.

7. F. Herzberg. "Motivation and productivity: Motivation through job enrichment." [film] Washington, D.C.: Bureau of National Affairs.

Chapter 16

1. J. Bacon. *Corporate directorship practices: Membership and committees of the board.* New York: National Industrial Conference Board, 1973.